C PROGRAMMING
Pocket Primer

C Programming

Pocket Primer

Oswald Campesato

MERCURY LEARNING AND INFORMATION

Dulles, Virginia
Boston, Massachusetts
New Delhi

Publisher: David Pallai
MERCURY LEARNING AND INFORMATION
22841 Quicksilver Drive
Dulles, VA 20166
info@merclearning.com
www.merclearning.com
800-232-0223

O. Campesato. *C Programming Pocket Primer.*
ISBN: 978-1-68392-388-6

The publisher recognizes and respects all marks used by companies, manufacturers, and developers as a means to distinguish their products. All brand names and product names mentioned in this book are trademarks or service marks of their respective companies. Any omission or misuse (of any kind) of service marks or trademarks, etc. is not an attempt to infringe on the property of others.

Library of Congress Control Number: 2018964991

192021321 This book is printed on acid-free paper in the United States of America.

Our titles are available for adoption, license, or bulk purchase by institutions, corporations, etc.

For additional information, please contact the Customer Service Dept. at
800-232-0223(toll free).

All of our titles are available in digital format at authorcloudware.com and other digital vendors. Companion files (figures and code listings) for this title are available by contacting info@merclearning.com. The sole obligation of MERCURY LEARNING AND INFORMATION to the purchaser is to replace the disc, based on defective materials or faulty workmanship, but not based on the operation or functionality of the product.

I'd like to dedicate this book to my parents –
may this bring joy and happiness into their lives.

CONTENTS

PREFACE

WHAT IS THE GOAL?

The goal of this book is to introduce advanced beginners to C programming fundamentals. Hence, the material is primarily for people who have some programming experience, and not really suitable for "absolute beginners." This book is suitable as a fast-paced introduction to various "core" features of C. The purpose of the material in the chapters is to illustrate how to solve a variety of tasks using C, after which you can do further reading to deepen your knowledge.

There is one other point to remember as you read this book: *this book will not make you an expert programmer in C.*

IS THIS BOOK IS FOR ME AND WHAT WILL I LEARN?

This book is intended for "beginner to intermediate" programmers with a year or two of experience in another language who wish to learn C. You need some familiarity with working from the command line in a Unix-like environment. However, there are subjective prerequisites, such as a strong desire to learn how to write C programs, along with the motivation and discipline to read and understand the code samples.

If you are adequately prepared and motivated, you will learn how to write C programs that involve various C data types, loops, conditional logic, built-in functions, custom functions, and recursion.

This book saves you the time required to search for relevant code samples, adapting them to your specific needs, which is a potentially time-consuming process. In any case, if you're not sure whether or not you can absorb the material in this book, glance through the code samples to get a feel for the level of complexity.

WHAT ARE THE STRENGTHS OF THIS BOOK?

The top three strengths of this book can be summarized as follows:

1. This is a modern textbook with up-to-date information regarding the C11 standard

2. There are detailed explanations of the code samples because nothing is assumed, which means that beginners can work through the examples side-by-side with the explanation

3. No assumptions regarding the level of programming skills of the readers

One other point to keep in mind: as you might have noticed, many introductory books are written assuming a computer science background: this book arguably is readable without that theoretical foundation.

WHAT ARE THE WEAKNESSES OF THIS BOOK?

The weaknesses of this book can be summarized as follows:

1. A thorough coverage of just the essentials of C in a book this short is difficult. You need to learn many details in order to become a good C programmer; hence, this book serves as a sort of "stepping" stone in your learning path regarding C.

2. The examples are necessarily simplistic, and cannot show the best style in a book for beginners because the best style is too complex to illustrate the simple concepts.

3. Some readers might find the introductory level of the material boring and simple. This is not a problem of the book, but the fact that C is so low-level that the foundations appear trivial. (They absolutely are not, but they look that way to a beginner.)

HOW WERE THE CODE SAMPLES CREATED?

The code samples in this book were created and tested using bash on a Macbook Pro with OS X 10.12.6 (macOS Sierra). Regarding their content: the code samples are derived primarily from the author, and in some cases there are code samples that incorporate short sections of code from discussions in online forums. The key point to remember is that the overwhelming majority of the code samples follow the "Four Cs": they must be Clear, Concise, Complete, and Correct to the extent that it's possible to do so, given the size of this book.

WHY ARE THERE TWO CHAPTERS ABOUT POINTERS IN C?

A misunderstanding of pointers is the most common cause of crashes in C programs. Although C pointers can be explained quickly, code samples involving pointers can quickly become difficult to understand (and also error-prone). This is a difficult subject (even for advanced beginners) if you are unfamiliar with this functionality. Hence, one chapter about C pointers simply isn't enough to become comfortable with this topic.

As you will see, Chapter 5 contains basic code samples involving pointers, which are enough for simple C programs. If you want a deeper understanding of how to use pointer, read the code samples in Chapter 6, and experiment with your own variations of the code. If you want to become adept in a programming language, you need to actively practice writing code, which is especially true for C programs that involve pointers.

WHICH TOPICS ARE EXCLUDED?

This book does not cover hashing, searching and sorting, file I/O, data structures, threads, sockets, IPC, pipes, shared memory, message queues, and other system-level functionality that are relevant for advanced and expert-level developers. These topics are excluded because they are not suitable for an introductory C book, and there are plenty of other concepts that you need to learn in order to write C programs. Note that Chapter 7 briefly covers bit manipulation and more sophisticated C operators that you will need to learn if you become a full-time C developer.

HOW DO I SET UP A COMMAND SHELL?

If you are a Mac user, there are three ways to do so. The first method is to use `Finder` to navigate to `Applications > Utilities` and then double click on the Utilities application. Next, if you already have a command shell available, you can launch a new command shell by typing the following command:

```
open /Applications/Utilities/Terminal.app
```

A second method for Mac users is to open a new command shell on a Macbook from a command shell that is already visible simply by clicking `command+n` in that command shell, and your Mac will launch another command shell.

If you are a PC user, you can install Cygwin (open source *https://cygwin. com/*) that simulates bash commands, or use another toolkit such as MKS (a commercial product). Please read the online documentation that describes the download and installation process. Note that custom aliases are not automatically set if they are defined in a file other than the main start-up file (such as .bash_login).

WHAT ARE THE "NEXT STEPS" AFTER FINISHING THIS BOOK?

The answer to this question varies widely, mainly because the answer depends heavily on your objectives. The best answer is to try a new tool or technique from the book on a problem or task you care about, professionally or personally. Precisely what that might be depends on who you are, as the needs of a data scientist, manager, student or developer are all different. In addition, keep what you learned in mind as you tackle new data cleaning or manipulation challenges. Sometimes knowing a technique is possible makes finding a solution easier, even if you have to re-read the section to remember exactly how the syntax works.

If you have reached the limits of what you have learned here and want to get further technical depth about regarding C, there are various online resources and literature describing more complex features of C.

Oswald Campesato
January 2019

ABOUT THE TECHNICAL EDITOR

Ansel Sermersheim has been working as a computer developer for nearly twenty years programming in C, C++, Lisp, Java, and Perl, with extensive knowledge in TCP/IP and multithreaded design. He has been a speaker at CppCon 2015, CppNow 2016, CppNow 2017, CppCon 2017, CppCon 2018, and numerous San Francisco Bay Area meetings of ACCU, the Association of C, and C++ Users.

Before college, he spent two years working at a start-up company developing a Java based real time data warehouse. During part of his time at college, he worked for NASA as a system administrator in a mixed environment including Windows, Linux, Solaris, OS X, and Irix. After receiving a degree in computer science, he worked at a communications company as a software engineer designing scalable, high performance, multi-threaded network daemons. Currently, he is an independent consultant.

He is one of the co-founders of CopperSpice, an open source C++ GUI library, and also the co-founder of DoxyPress which is an open source program used to generate documentation from code written in C, C++, and several other languages. He is the primary developer of libGuarded which is an open source library for managing access to shared data in multithreaded C++ applications.

For more information about the CopperSpice project, please visit www.copperspice.com or www.youtube.com/copperspice.

Ansel Sermersheim
email: ansel@copperspice.com

## CHAPTER 1

INTRODUCTION TO C

Since this book is for advanced beginners, the first chapter contains topics that will prepare you to compile and execute simple C programs. Consequently, the coverage of the historical details regarding C is sparse: they rarely help you to learn in C, and if you are really interested, you can find those details in various online articles. Moreover, this chapter does not contain all the minutiae of C because they simply are not necessary in an introductory C programming book (besides, you will learn those details on an as-needed basis if you become a full-time C programmer).

Stated in simple terms, the goal of this chapter is to make its contents as useful and relevant as the other chapters in this book (i.e., no filler material just because it's Chapter 1). In particular, this chapter starts with the rudimentary aspects of C and also shows you how to create, compile, and execute a C program, all of which is discussed in the first half of the chapter.

Although this chapter contains a mixture of topics, the flow of the technical material is essentially sequential and logically structured. The non-sequential code samples contain C features before they are formally introduced. Fortunately, the purpose of those out-of-sequence features is clear: for example, the printf() function is obviously for printing things.

So, although the code samples in this book minimize "forward referencing" technical details, it's sometimes a good way to make the code samples more interesting and useful. For instance, the section about for loops in Chapter 2 contains conditional logic (even though if/else statements are discussed later in that chapter) in order to present more meaningful code samples that are still easy to understand.

With all the preceding points in mind, let's quickly go over the major sections of this chapter. The first part briefly discusses some of the command-line tools that are available for C programs, such as gcc (required), make (optional and discussed in the Appendix), and lint (also optional), as well as an editor for creating C source code. This section also discusses the location of other "standard" files that you will often use in your C programs.

The second portion of this chapter contains a brief introduction to the C programming language, along with some advantages of C, some of the available versions of C, and an overview of the structure of C programs. You will also see a "hello world" program in C and how to compile this program from the command line.

The third portion of this chapter discusses data types in C, binary and ternary operators, and naming conventions for variables in C programs. The next portion contains code samples with alphabetic types and how to calculate mathematical quantities, such as ceiling values, floor values, absolute values, and trigonometric values in C.

The fourth part of this chapter contains a brief introduction to arrays in C and how to add the numbers in an array. This section provides a sort of segue into Chapter 2 (which contains details and code samples about arrays) as well as Chapter 5 (which contains examples of C arrays and pointers).

After you complete the smorgasbord of topics in this chapter, you will be in a good position to absorb the material in the remaining chapters of this book.

COMMAND LINE TOOLS

Although the lower-level details of compiling, linking, and loading a program are important, you can learn how to compile C programs with just a few details. This section describes various command line tools, some of which are optional (at least for now).

The gcc Compiler

The gcc utility compiles C programs and generates an executable file that you can launch from the command line. This utility has many options, and the one that we need for the code samples in this book is the "-o" option. Use this option in order to specify the name of the executable file to create after having compiled the relevant C program(s).

For example, if you have a C program called MyTest.c, you can create the executable MyTest with the following command: (the switch -std=c11 is discussed in Chapter 2):

```
gcc -std=c11 MyTest.c -o MyTest
```

If you do not already have gcc on your Mac, you can register for a free Apple account and, in the Apple developer page, click the "Developer Tools" checkbox and download the dmg file in the "Command Line Tools for Xcode" option. After launching the dmg file to install gcc, invoke the following command from the command line:

```
gcc -v
```

If `gcc` is installed correctly, you will see output similar to the following:

```
Using built-in specs.
COLLECT_GCC=gcc
COLLECT_LTO_WRAPPER=/opt/local/libexec/gcc/x86_64-
  apple-darwin16/7.2.0/lto-wrapper
Target: x86_64-apple-darwin16
Configured with:
/opt/local/var/macports/build/_opt_bblocal_var_buildworker_
ports_build_ports_lang_gcc7/gcc7/work/gcc-7.2.0/configure
--prefix=/opt/local --build=x86_64-apple-darwin16
--enable-languages=c,c++,objc,obj-c++,lto,fortran
--libdir=/opt/local/lib/gcc7
gcc version 7.2.0 (MacPorts gcc7 7.2.0_0)
```

The code samples in this book use the GNU `gcc` compiler, and in case you don't already have it on your machine, you can download the compiler for your platform here:

https://gcc.gnu.org/releases.html

Useful Switches for the `gcc` Command (optional)

Some of these switches might not make sense right now, but they are presented in one location so that you can refer to them in case you need them for code samples in later chapters.
Check for C11 compliance with the `-std` switch:

```
gcc -std=c11 -o test test.c
```

Display all warning messages with the `-Wall` switch:

```
gcc -std=c11 -Wall -o test test.c
```

Create an object file with the `-o` switch:

```
gcc -std=c11 -o test test.c
```

Create an assembly file with the `-S` switch:

```
gcc -std=c11 -S test.c
```

Include debugging information with the `-g` switch:

```
gcc -std=c11 -g test.c
```

If you decide later to remove debugging information, then either recompile without the `-g` switch or use the `strip` command.
Display all options applied at each compilation step with the `-v` switch:

```
gcc -std=c11 -v test.c
```

Specify the path `/usr/lib/` with the `-L` switch:

```
gcc -std=c11 -L/usr/lib test.c -o test
```

Display help information for `gcc`:

```
gcc -help
```

There are also environment variables for the `gcc` command, such as `TMPDIR`, which specifies the location of a temporary directory. An example of the value for the `TMPDIR` variable is here:

```
/var/folders/3g/4s50gz4d22147815q8jz6gzm0000gn/T/
```

Perform an online search to find out about other environment variables for the `gcc` command.

The `lint`-related Utilities (optional)

The original `lint` utility checked C programs for syntax irregularities and provides various types of warning messages. For example, the `printf()` function has a return type called `int` (return types are discussed in Chapter 4). Thus, `lint` generates a warning message for the following code snippet because the return value of the `printf()` function is "unused":

```
printf("%s\n", "Hello World");
```

In earlier versions of C, the way to avoid a `lint` warning message was to use the following syntax:

```
(void)printf("%s\n", "Hello World");
```

However, the `lint` utility is quite old, and modern compilers will catch many coding anomalies that were previously handled by `lint`. In case you're interested, there are `lint`-like tools available that you can install and analyze your code (perform an Internet search for such tools).

One such tool is `splint`, which supports most of the C99 standard (discussed in Chapter 2), and it's downloadable here:

http://www.splint.org/

Another tool is `cppcheck`, which works on C code as well as C++ code, and you can install this utility on Mac with this command:

```
brew install cppcheck
```

Note that `cppcheck` does not report a warning even if the return value of the `printf()` function is unused. More details regarding `cppcheck` are here:

http://cppcheck.sourceforge.net/

Incidentally, if you hear people using the term "linter," they are referring to a tool that analyzes source code to find various anomalies, such as programming errors, syntax errors, and other irregularities.

Editors and IDEs

The code samples in this book were written with the `vim` editor, which is available on all Unix/Linux machines, but you can use any text editor that's convenient for you.

In addition, there are IDEs available, but they aren't necessary for the code samples in this book. If you prefer an IDE, `Code::Block` is a reasonable choice, or you can try Eclipse or NetBeans.

Now that you have an understanding of the tools for creating and compiling C programs, and also some optional command-line tools, let's look at the C programming language, the topic of the next section.

WHAT IS C?

C is an imperative programming language with a static type system. C "maps" efficiently to machine instructions and is sometimes called "a high level assembly language." In fact, C appears in operating systems and in computers from embedded systems to supercomputers.

Dennis Ritchie developed C at Bell Labs (between 1969 and 1973), and it forms the foundation of the Unix operating system. In addition, C was standardized by the American National Standards Institute (ANSI) in 1989 (ANSI C) and subsequently by the International Organization for Standardization (ISO).

Compiled C provides low-level access to memory and required minimal run-time support, and it was intended to encourage cross-platform programming. Indeed, portably written C programs can be compiled on a wide variety of computer platforms and operating systems with minor changes to the C code.

C is a compact yet intricate low-level language that requires a non-trivial amount of effort to learn well. For instance, C supports different sizes of integer variables, along with an intricate set of low-level operators. As another example, C supports Unicode (discussed briefly in Chapter 7), whose rules and exceptions are more complex than other languages.

What is Special About C?

C is the language of systems programming, and various operating systems have been written in C (albeit with portions of assembly code as well). C is also the language of small microcontrollers. Moreover, C provides you with a glimpse into the internal workings of a computer that's not possible in other, high-level languages. You might be surprised to discover that the Java and Python virtual machines were initially implemented as C programs, and then they are compiled from C code to binaries.

Incidentally, the C++ language (which is an extension of C) is also a low-level structured programming language. You can create a C `struct` (a data type that is discussed in Chapter 7) whose memory layout matches the physical hardware registers on a particular device, which is very useful when writing operating system device drivers (and not possible in the vast majority of other languages).

Although this book is about C and not C++, here is a short list of uses for C++, just in case you are interested:

- Web browsers
- robotics
- games
- device drivers
- hardware controllers
- low level mathematics
- office applications
- graphics editors
- operating systems

Hence, if your intent is to write programs that can handle lower-level tasks, then it's definitely worth the effort to learn how to write C programs.

Major Revisions to C

This book does not discuss versions of C prior to the C99 ISO standard, which was released in 1999. Note that earlier versions of the C language include K&R C, ANSI C, and C90. The C99 standard incorporates many new features, such as:

- inline functions
- new data types (such as long long int and a complex type)
- variable-length arrays and flexible array members
- improved support for IEEE 754 floating point
- support for variadic macros (macros that take a variable number of arguments)
- support for one-line comments beginning with //

While C99 is mostly backward compatible with C90, keep in mind that there are some restrictions.

A more recent major revision (starting around 2007) of the C standard is called C11, which adds numerous new features, including:

- type generic macros
- anonymous structures
- improved Unicode support
- atomic operations
- multi-threading
- bounds-checked functions
- improved compatibility with C++

C11 makes some portions of the existing C99 library optional.

NOTE *Chapter 2 contains information about checking your source code for compliance with the rules of the C11 standard.*

Yet another revision involved embedded C programming, which previously required non-standard extensions to the C language in order to support features such as fixed-point arithmetic, multiple distinct memory banks, and basic I/O operations. Then in 2008 the C Standards Committee extended the C language to provide a common standard for adherence by all implementations. These additional features include fixed-point arithmetic, named address spaces, and basic I/O hardware addressing.

A HIGH-LEVEL VIEW OF C PROGRAMS

This section briefly discusses the structure of C programs, coding guidelines, and keywords in C. The information in the following subsections will become more meaningful as you gain practice writing C programs, so it's worth revisiting this section after you have read several chapters in this book.

The Structure of C Programs

As you will see in the code samples in this book, a C program can contain a combination of the following:

- comments (Chapter 2)
- statements/expressions (Chapter 2)
- variables (Chapter 2)
- if-else conditional logic (Chapter 2)
- for/while/do loops (Chapter 2)
- functions (Chapter 4)
- preprocessor commands (Chapter 7)

If you have some coding experience, you might already be familiar with conditional logic, loops, and functions. However, preprocessor commands are probably new to you, and they are discussed in Chapter 7.

Coding Guidelines

Simple and clear programs, with appropriately commented code blocks, are preferred because they will be easier to understand, debug, and enhance (as a general rule). Some guidelines include:

1. Keep functions (discussed in Chapter 4) short and meaningful
2. Each function has one primary purpose
3. Avoid complex logic involving multiple nested if-blocks
4. Avoid comment code blocks that are complex or non-intuitive
5. Avoid commenting every line of code

Keep in mind that the preceding rules are intended as general guidelines and they can be broken if it increases code clarity (but try to do so sparingly).

Keywords in C

The C language supports a set of keywords that you cannot use as variables in C programs: if you attempt to do so, your code will not compile correctly. Some of these keywords appear in other languages, and some of them are specific to C.

Here is an extensive (though not necessarily complete) list of keywords in C (in no particular order): `auto`, `double`, `int`, `struct`, `break`, `else`, `long`, `switch`, `case`, `enum`, `register`, `typedef`, `char`, `extern`, `return`, `union`, `const`, `float`, `short`, `unsigned`, `continue`, `for`, `signed`, `void`, `default`, `goto`, `sizeof`, `volatile`, `do`, `if`, `static`, `while`, `inline`, `restrict`, `_Bool`, `_Complex`, and `_Imaginary`.

The C11 keywords include: `_Alignas`, `_Alignof`, `_Atomic`, `_Generic`, `_Noreturn`, `_Static_assert`, and `_Thread_local`.

At this point you have just enough background information about C to create a simple "Hello World" program. This code sample is the first step toward creating interesting and useful C programs that involve data types, variables, conditional logic, and so forth.

Before we proceed, don't forget to have `gcc` installed on your machine (type `which gcc` from the command line to see the location of `gcc`), which you'll need in order to compile your C programs. Now let's proceed to the next section, which explains how to create, compile, and launch a simple C program.

A HELLO WORLD PROGRAM IN C

As mentioned earlier in this chapter, sometimes you will see C functions (such as the `printf()` function) introduced in C programs before they are fully explained. However, such functions are usually intuitive and easy to comprehend, and they are also explained in greater detail later in the chapter.

With the preceding point in mind, Listing 1.1 displays the contents of `HelloWorld.c`, which is a minimalistic C program that illustrates how to use the `printf()` function to display the string "Hello World" on the command line.

LISTING 1.1: HelloWorld.c
```c
#include <stdio.h>

int main()
{
    printf("Hello World\n");

    return 0;
}
```

The first line in Listing 1.1 is probably obscure: it's an "include" statement (which is *always* preceded by the "#" symbol), which refers to the file stdio.h (commonly called a "header" file). Many C programs include this header file, which contains something called the "prototype" definition of the printf() function (as well as many other functions). Let's defer the lengthy details regarding header files until the next section; for now we can gloss over the details and just discuss the rest of Listing 1.1.

As you can see, the remaining portion of Listing 1.1 is straightforward: there is a function called main() that takes no arguments and returns a value of type int. Inside the main() function there are two simple lines of code. The first line is the printf() function that prints the string "Hello World." (we'll look at the printf() function in more detail later). The second line is a return statement that returns the value 0 because that's the return type of the main() function. Some people think that it's unnecessary to include an explicit "return 0" statement in the main() function, whereas others think the additional line of code involves minimal extra effort.

Believe it or not, you have just completed your first C program! If you're impatient, you can skip the next several sections (but make sure you do read them at some point) and go to the section that explains how to compile this C program.

C Header Files and Libraries

By convention, header files in C programs are named with the suffix ".h" (and .hpp extensions are very common for header files for C++ programs). The header file stdio.h that you saw in Listing 1.1 is physically located in the directory /usr/lib/include, which is the location of many other standard header files. In addition to standard header files you can also define your own custom header files, which is discussed briefly in Chapter 7.

In addition to header files, there are some binary files called "library" files that are automatically included when you compile a C program. The directory /usr/lib is the standard location for many standard library files that are available as part of the C programming environment (and yes, you can also create custom libraries, but this topic is beyond the scope of this book).

In case you're wondering, it is also possible to specify additional "header" files and libraries from the command line, as well as inside a so-called "makefile." The Appendix contains more information about make files.

Valid Syntax for the main() Function

The main() function in Listing 1.1 has the simplest valid format that complies with C11, and at this point it's the easiest format to explain. The following declarations of the main() function are valid in C11:

- int main(void)
- int main()

- `int main(int argc, char **argv)`
- `int main(int argc, char *argv[])`

The third and fourth declarations in the preceding list involve pointers, which are discussed in Chapter 5 and Chapter 6. Another point to keep in mind is that the following format is valid in some operating systems:

```
int main(int argc, char **argv, char **envp)
```

The fourth code snippet contains a third parameter envp that "points" to the environment (i.e., the environment variables) where a C program is launched. However, you can access and update environment variables via getenv() and putenv(), respectively, which are discussed in Chapter 6.

If you want to specify command line arguments that are accessible inside a C program, you need to use the following syntax (which is a commonly used syntax):

```
int main(int argc, char **argv)
```

The first argument argc is a number that equals the number of command line arguments. The second argument argv in the preceding snippet is a pointer-to-a-pointer, which we'll see in a later chapter. Note that you can use the preceding syntax in Listing 1.1 and the code compilation is performed in the same manner.

C Program Syntax

There are several conventions for placing curly braces in C programs, and the comments in this section are generally applicable to code blocks in C. We'll use the code in Listing 1.1 as a simple illustration for program syntax. Depending on your preference, you can place the initial curly brace in Listing 1.1 on the same line, as shown here:

```
int main() {
    printf("Hello World\n");
}
```

In fact, you can even use the following syntax (not recommended in order to maintain code readability):

```
int main() { printf("Hello World\n"); }
```

COMPILING C PROGRAMS

The compilation process involves converting C programs into "object" files, which are files that contain binary code (such files have a ".o" extension). In this book the code samples involve a single C program (Chapter 7 discusses how to compile multiple custom C programs), so the compilation step is straightforward.

After the compilation step, the object file is automatically "assembled" with other files, such as library files (discussed earlier in this chapter). The result of this process is an executable file that you can launch from the command line.

In case you're wondering, there are several C compilers available for Unix, Linux, and OS X. The original C compiler is cc, and an open source version of this C compiler is gcc. You can check for the presence of these compilers as follows:

```
$ which cc
/usr/bin/cc
$ which gcc
/opt/local/bin/gcc
```

This book uses gcc to compile C programs, and an invocation of the gcc compiler that compiles the program in Listing 1.1 is shown here:

```
gcc -std=c11 HelloWorld.c -o HelloWorld
```

Provided that there were no compilation errors, the preceding command generates the following executable:

```
HelloWorld
```

Now launch the preceding executable with this command:

```
./HelloWorld
```

The output is here:

```
Hello World
```

Note that you can also compile the program in Listing 1.1 without the -o switch, as shown here:

```
gcc HelloWorld.c
```

The preceding command generates the following executable:

```
a.out
```

You can launch the preceding executable by invoking a.out from the command line and you will see the same output. In fact, you can specify any legitimate filename with the -o switch, but it's customary to specify the name of the source file without its suffix (in this case it's HelloWorld).

Moreover, C programs can have dependencies on other C programs (written by you or someone else), and you can include these C programs on the command line. For example, if the C program main1.c depends on the C programs depend1.c and depend2.c, you can use the make utility (discussed in the Appendix) to specify these dependencies and ensure that they are compiled and linked to create the binary file main1.

VARIABLE NAMES IN C

Variables in C must be defined in a declaration statement that contains 1) the name of the variable and 2) the type of the variable. The value of the variable is optional. Variable declarations in C programs can appear before the `main()` code block, inside the `main()` function, or inside user-defined functions. Some developers think it's better to define variables at the top of a function or near the block of code where they are used. Although opinions differ, the latter is common among object-oriented programming languages such as C++.

As a simple example, the following code snippet declares (but does not initialize) one variable of type integer, followed by a declaration of a second variable of type integer that is also initialized with an integer value:

```
int myInt1;
int myInt2 = 7;
```

Notice that variable declarations end with a semicolon. You can also define multiple variables of the same type in a single statement, as shown here:

```
int myInt1, myInt2 = 7, myInt3 = 25;
```

The general form of a variable declaration is:

```
type name; /* comment */
```

where `type` is one of the C variable types (int, float, etc.) and `name` is any valid variable name in C.

Assignment Statements

Assignment statements are used to give a value to a variable. The following code snippet is a very simple example of an assignment statement:

```
num = (1 + 2) * 4;
```

The variable `num` on the left side of the equals operator (=) is declared earlier in a C program (not shown here) and assigned the value of the expression (1 + 2) * 4, so the variable `num` is assigned the value 12.

The general form of the assignment statement in C is:

```
variable = expression ;
```

The = sign is used for assignment, and it literally means: compute the value of `expression` and assign the value of `expression` to the variable on the left side of the equals sign.

NOTE
Chapter 2 discusses global variables, local variables, and formal parameters.

INDENTATION AND CODE FORMAT

Use indentation to make programs easier to understand (for you as well as other people). C programs indent one level for each new block or conditional. There are two popular styles of indentation: one style places the initial curly brace on the same line as the code and the other style places the initial curly brace on a separate line.

Although you can probably guess the purpose of an if/else code block and a while statement, let's wait until Chapter 2 to delve into the meaning of the next set of code blocks and merely view the code from the standpoint of the indentation style. With that in mind, here is an example of the first indentation style:

```
if (total <= 0) {
    printf("You owe nothing\n");
    total = 0;
} else {
    printf("You owe %d dollars\n", total);
    all_totals = all_totals + total;
}
```

Notice that the initial curly brace in the preceding block is on the same line as the if and else keywords. The following code block illustrates the second style of indentation:

```
while (! done)
{
    printf("Processing\n");
    next_entry();
}

if (total <= 0)
{
    printf("You owe nothing\n");
    total = 0;
}
else
{
    printf("You owe %d dollars \n", total);
    all_totals = all_totals + total;
}
```

Use the format that you prefer (if you have a choice), unless you are required to follow a different coding convention in your organization. Since you will encounter both formats in C programs, it's worthwhile becoming comfortable with both styles.

One more detail: indentation is typically two or four spaces, and the use of tabs is discouraged because the way that tabs are treated depends on the text editors. Consistency is more important than the size of indentation.

THE PRINTF() FUNCTION

In Listing 1.1 you saw an example of using the printf() function in order to print a text string. The values of other types of variables are also printed using the printf() function, which uses formats to match different data types. In particular, the formats %c, %d, and %f specify a character, an integer, and a floating point number, respectively. In addition, there is a "family" of functions whose semantics are similar to the printf() function, such as the sprintf() function for putting data in a buffer and fprintf() function for printing data to a file.

C supports the following output formatting:

```
%d      // print as decimal integer
%6d     // print as decimal integer, at least 6 characters
        wide
%f      // print as floating point
%6f     // print as floating point, at least 6 characters
        wide
%.2f    // print as floating point, 2 characters after
        decimal point
%6.2f   // print as floating point, at least 6 wide and 2
        after decimal point
```

The printf() function also recognizes %o for octal, %x for hexadecimal, %c for character, %s for character string, and %% for % itself (numbers in octal and hexadecimal are discussed later).

Listing 1.2 displays the contents of IntExample.c that illustrates how to initialize an integer-valued variable and then use the printf() function to display arithmetic operations on that variable.

LISTING 1.2: IntExample.c

```c
#include <stdio.h>

int term; /* term used in two expressions */

int main()
{
  term = 3 * 5;

  printf("Twice %d is %d\n", term, 2*term);
  printf("Three times %d is %d\n", term, 3*term);

  return (0);
}
```

Listing 1.2 contains a main() method that declares and initializes the variable term with the value 15. The first printf() statement contains two %d conversions in order to display the values of term and 2*term, respectively. The second printf() statement also contains two %d conversions in order to display the values of term and 3*term, respectively.

Hence, every %d conversion must have a corresponding value to display, and vice versa. The same is true for other conversions, such as %f. Also keep in mind that extraneous expressions are ignored, and if too few expressions are specified, the results are unpredictable. Although the GNU gcc compiler checks printf() arguments, try not to rely on this feature.

DATA TYPES IN C

We have already seen some of the primitive data types in C, such as int, double, and float. Later in this chapter you will see a C program that illustrates how to print an assortment of primitive numeric data types.

C also supports a character type (but not a string type), as well as arrays that can contain primitive types. Later in this chapter you will see code samples that contain characters, strings, and arrays.

By way of illustration, C supports the following data types (with examples in parentheses):

```
int      // integer (ex: 8)
float    // floating point (ex: 5.1234)
char     // character (ex: 'a')
short    // short integer
long     // long integer
double   // double-precision floating point
```

In addition to the preceding list of primitive data types, C supports pointers, which is a very powerful feature that is unavailable in many languages (such as Java). C pointers are actually a family of pointer data types. Whenever you declare a pointer, you must also specify what kind of data it will point to in order to form a concrete data type.

In fact, a C pointer can point to more complex built-in data types (such as a C struct) as well as custom data types. The concept of pointers will become clearer in Chapter 5 and Chapter 6, which delve into the details about pointers (along with code samples).

The sizeof() Operator in C

The built-in sizeof() operator is an easy way to determine the amount of memory (number of bytes) that are allocated to a variable or a structure (built-in structures and custom structures are discussed in Chapter 7).

Listing 1.3 displays the contents of SizeOfDataType.c that illustrates how to use the sizeof() function to determine the storage allocated to various data types in C.

LISTING 1.3: SizeOfDataTypes.c

```
#include <stdio.h>

int main()
{
```

```
char state[] = "California";

printf("Size of char:    %lu\n", sizeof(char));
printf("Size of int:     %lu\n", sizeof(int));
printf("Size of float:   %lu\n", sizeof(float));
printf("Size of double:  %lu\n", sizeof(double));
printf("Size of state:   %lu\n", sizeof(state));

return (0);
}
```

Listing 1.3 contains a main() function that initializes the character array state with a hard-coded string. The remaining portion of code consists of 4 printf() statements that display the number of bytes for char, int, float, and double data types in C. The final printf() statement displays the number of bytes occupied by the character string state. The output from launching the C program in Listing 1.3 is here:

```
Size of char:    1
Size of int:     4
Size of float:   4
Size of double:  8
Size of state:   11
```

OPERATORS IN C

The C programming language provides operators that can be classified into several categories, including arithmetic operators, increment/decrement operators, and ternary operators. The following subsections provide more details about each type of operator.

Arithmetic Operators

Arithmetic operators are "+", "-", "*", and "/" for addition, subtraction, multiplication, and division, respectively. Arithmetic operators have the following precedence levels in expressions that do not contain parentheses:
* and / have the same level (left-to-right if both appear)
+ and – have the same level (left-to-right if both appear)
Parentheses can override the default precedence levels (and can also be nested). The main purpose of parentheses is to alter the default order of execution in expressions that contain arithmetic operators, as shown here:

```
7-5+8 = 2+8 = 10 (left-to-right precedence)
7-(5+8) = 7 - 13 = -6
3*8/4 = 24/4 = 6 (left-to-right precedence)
3*(8/4) = 3*2 = 6
```

When in doubt, use parentheses in an expression. For example, the expression 8*x+y*z/10 is the same as (8*x)+(y*z)/10, but the latter is clearer.

Another arithmetic operator is the modulus % operator, which provides the integer remainder from dividing an integer by a non-zero integer:

```
7 % 4 = 3
10 % 10 = 0
```

Exponentiation has the highest precedence, except when overridden by parentheses, as shown here:

```
2**4-3 = 16-3 = 13
2**(4-3) = 2**1 = 2
```

Listing 1.4 displays the contents of `Arithmetic.c` that illustrates how to perform arithmetic operations.

LISTING 1.4: Arithmetic.c

```c
#include <stdio.h>

int main()
{
    int x = 5 + 3;
    int y = 5 - 3;
    int z = 5 * 3;
    int w = 5 / 3;

    printf("5 + 3 = %d\n",x);
    printf("5 - 3 = %d\n",y);
    printf("5 * 3 = %d\n",z);
    printf("5 / 3 = %d\n",w);

    return (0);
}
```

Listing 1.4 contains a `main()` function that initializes 4 integer variables x, y, z, and w, followed by 4 `printf()` statements that display the values of those same variables. The output from launching the C program in Listing 1.4 is here:

```
5 + 3 = 8
5 - 3 = 2
5 * 3 = 15
5 / 3 = 1
```

Increment/Decrement Operators

In C there are two ways to increment or decrement a variable by 1. One way is shown in the following code block:

```c
int a=5, b=9;
a += 1;
b -= 1;
```

After the preceding code block has executed, a has the value 6 and b has the value 8. However, the preceding construct cannot be combined with the `==` operator: you must first perform the increment or decrement operation, and *then* you can perform the `if` logic.

The second way is to use the increment and decrement operators, which are ++ and --, respectively. When these operators appear on the *left* side of a variable, the increment or decrement operation is performed *before* any other operations. However, when these operators appear on the *right* side of a variable, the increment or decrement operation is performed *after* other arithmetic operations. The following code block illustrates these points:

```
int x=0, y=1;
if(++x == 1) { //first add 1 to x and then compare (this is
              true)
             // do something
}

if(y++ == 1) { //first compare and then add 1 to y (this is
              true)
             //do something
}
```

After the preceding code block is executed, x has the value 1 and y has the value 2, and *both* if statements are executed.

Now consider the following code block, where x and y are initialized with the values 6 and 2, respectively:

```
int x=6, y=2;
if(--x == 6) { //subtract 1 from x and then compare (this
              is false)
             // do something
}

if(y++ == 3) { //first compare then add 1 to y (this is
              false)
             // do something
}
```

After the preceding pair of if statements are executed, x is equal to 5 and y is equal to 3, but *neither* if statement is executed (compare this result with the previous pair of if statements).

Ternary Operator

A ternary operator is a short-hand way of performing if/else conditional logic. As a simple example, consider the following code block:

```
if (a < b)
{
    x = 1;
}
else
{
    x = 2;
}
```

The preceding code snippet can be represented in a more abstract conditional form as follows:

```
if (expr1)
{
    expr2;
}
else
{
    expr3;
}
```

Another way to simplify the preceding if/else logic is via the ternary operator that has the following form:

```
expr1 ? expr2 : expr3
```

For example, the code block at the beginning of this section can be expressed as follows:

```
x = (a<b ? 1 : 2);
```

In the preceding code snippet, if the inequality a<b is true, then x is assigned the value 1; otherwise, x is assigned the value 2.

The next portion of this chapter contains code samples that illustrate how to use built-in C functions to calculate the ceiling and the floor of a number, the absolute value of a number, and some trigonometric functions. Chapter 4 provides additional built-in C functions (and then shows you how to define custom functions in C).

CALCULATING CEILING AND FLOOR VALUES

C provides various built-in functions that perform arithmetic and mathematical calculations, such as the ceil() function and the floor() function. Listing 1.5 displays the contents of MathValues.c that illustrates how to calculate the ceiling and the floor of decimal values.

LISTING 1.5: MathValues.c

```
#include <math.h>
#include <stdio.h>

int main()
{
    double y, z;

    y = ceil(1.05);         // y = 2.0
    z = ceil(-1.05);        // z = -1.0
    printf("y = %.2f ; z = %.2f\n", y, z);

    y = floor(2.8);
```

```
z = floor(-2.8);
printf("y = %.2f ; z = %.2f\n", y, z);

return 0;
}
```

Listing 1.5 contains a main() function that initializes the variables y and z with two invocations of the built-in ceil() function in C. Next, a printf() statement displays the values of z and y, and then y and z are assigned different values by invoking the built-in floor() function in C, after which their values are displayed. The output from compiling and executing the code in Listing 1.5 is here:

```
The absolute value of x1 is 4.
fabs( -11.230000 ) = 11.230000
```

CALCULATING ABSOLUTE VALUES

C provides built-in functions that perform arithmetic calculations on floating point numbers, such as the fabs() function. Listing 1.6 displays the contents of AbsValues.c that illustrates how to calculate the absolute values of integers and decimal values.

LISTING 1.6: AbsValues.c

```
#include <math.h>
#include <stdlib.h>
#include <stdio.h>

int main()
{
    int x1 = -4, y1;
    double x2=-11.23,y2;

    y1 = abs(x1);
    printf("The absolute value of x1 is %d\n", y1);

    y2 = fabs(x2);
    printf("fabs( %lf ) = %lf\n", x2, y2);

    return 0;
}
```

Listing 1.6 contains a main() function that initializes the variables x1, y1, and y2. The variables y1 and y2 are initialized via functions calls to the built-in functions abs() and fabs(), respectively. Two printf() statements display the values of x1, y1, x2, and y2. The output from compiling and executing the code in Listing 1.6 is here:

```
The absolute value of x1 is 4.
fabs( -11.230000 ) = 11.230000
```

CALCULATING TRIGONOMETRIC VALUES IN C

C also provides built-in functions that perform trigonometric calculations. Listing 1.7 displays the contents of `TrigValues.c` that illustrates how to use the `sin()`, `cos()`, and `tan()` function return the value of the sine, cosine, and tangent of x, respectively.

LISTING 1.7: TrigValues.c

```
#include <math.h>
#include <stdio.h>

#define PI 3.1415926535

int main()
{
    double pi, x, y1, y2, y3;

    x = PI/4;
    y1 = sin(x);
    y2 = cos(x);
    y3 = tan(x);

    printf("sin( %lf ) = %lf\n", x, y1);
    printf("cos( %lf ) = %lf\n", x, y2);
    printf("tan( %lf ) = %lf\n", x, y3);

    return 0;
}
```

Listing 1.7 contains a `main()` function that initializes the variable x to PI/4, and then initializes the variables y1, y2, and y3 via invocations of the built-in C functions `sin()`, `cos()`, and `tan()`, respectively. Three `printf()` statements display the values of y1, y2, and y3. The output from compiling and executing the code in Listing 1.7 is here:

```
sin( 0.785398 ) = 0.707107
cos( 0.785398 ) = 0.707107
tan( 0.785398 ) = 1.000000
```

WORKING WITH DIFFERENT BASES IN C

Integer and decimal numbers are base 10 by default, but you can work with other bases, such as binary, octal, and hexadecimal. Listing 1.8 displays the contents of `OtherBases.c` that contains an assortment of code snippets that illustrate how to work with numbers in binary, octal, and hexadecimal in C.

Please keep the following caveat in mind: binary integer literals are a feature of C++14, and not in any C standard. Although binary integers are a nonstandard GCC extension in C, this feature can be useful with you need to perform bit-level operations (discussed in Chapter 7).

LISTING 1.8: OtherBases.c

```
#include <stdio.h>

// binary values start with 0b:
int a=0b0101; // decimal value is 5

// octal values start with 0:
int b=016;      // decimal value is 14

// hex values start with 0x or 0X:
int x1=0x18, x2=0X37, x3=0xAB;

int main()
{
   int a1=0b0101, b1=0x16, c1=123;
   int x1=0x18, x2=0X37, x3=0xAB;

   printf("a1=%d b2=%d c3=%d\n",a1, b1, c1);
   printf("x1=%d x2=%d x3=%d\n",x1, x2, x3);

   return 0;
}
```

Listing 1.8 first initializes the variables a1 and b1 to binary and octal values, respectively. The next code snippet initializes the variables x1, x2, and x3 to hexadecimal values. Note that all these variables are global variables.

The next section of code is a main() function that initializes the local variables a1, b2, and c1 to binary, hexadecimal, and integer values, respectively. The final section of code is two printf() statements that display the values of all these variables. The output from compiling and executing the code in Listing 1.8 is here:

```
a1=5 b2=22 c3=123
x1=24 x2=55 x3=171
```

Now let's take a brief look at char types and arrays in C programs, as a prelude to some of the code samples that you will see in Chapter 2.

WORKING WITH THE CHAR TYPE IN C

Listing 1.9 displays the contents of ReverseChars.c that illustrates how to initialize three characters and then print them in "reverse" order.

Listing 1.9: ReverseChars.c

```
#include <stdio.h>

char char1; char char2; char char3;

int main()
{
```

```
// first character
char1 = 'A';

// second character
char2 = 'B';

// third character
char3 = 'C';

printf("%c%c%c reversed is %c%c%c\n",
       char1, char2, char3,
       char3, char2, char1);

return (0);
}
```

Compile the code and launch the executable and you will see the following output:

```
ABC reversed is CBA
```

Now that we've seen code samples with simple built-in C functions, let's learn about arrays and strings in C, which are the topics in the rest of this chapter.

WHAT ARE C ARRAYS?

This section provides a very short introduction to C arrays, as a sort of preview before delving into the details about arrays in Chapter 2.

An "array" is a set of consecutive memory locations used to store data. Each item in the array is called an "element." The number of elements in an array is called the "dimension" of the array. A typical array declaration is shown here:

```
int mylist[3];
```

The preceding code snippet declares `mylist` as an array of three elements, which you can access via `mylist[0]`, `mylist[1]`, and `mylist[2]`. Notice that the first element has an index value of 0, the second element has an index value of 1, and so forth. Thus, if you declare an array of 100 elements, then the 100th element has index value of 99.

NOTE   *The first position in a C array has index 0.*

Now that you have a basic understanding of how to declare an array, let's see how to declare and initialize an array of decimal numbers and compute the sum of those numbers, as discussed in the next section.

ADDING THE NUMBERS IN AN ARRAY

Listing 1.10 displays the contents of `AddArray.c` that illustrates how to compute the total and the average value of the numbers in an integer-valued array (and in Chapter 2 we will use a loop).

LISTING 1.10: AddArray.c

```c
#include <stdio.h>

float data[5]; // data to average and total
float total;   // the total of the data items
float average; // average of the items

int main()
{
   data[0] = 34.0;
   data= 27.0;
   data= 45.0;
   data= 82.0;
   data[4] = 22.0;

   total = data[0] + data[1] + data[2] + data+ data[4];
   average = total / 5.0;
   printf("Total %f Average %f \n", total, average);

   return (0);
}
```

Listing 1.10 starts by declaring the variables `data`, `total`, and `average` as `float` variables. The next section is the `main()` function that initializes the 5 values of the `data` array. The variable `total` is initialized with the sum of the values in the `data` array, followed by the variable `average` that is the average of the numbers in the `data` array. The last code snippet displays the values of the variables `total` and `average`.

Compile the code in Listing 1.10 as follows:

```
gcc -std=c11 AddArray.c -o AddArray
```

Now launch the binary executable and you will see the following output:

```
Total 210.000000 Average 42.000000
```

SUMMARY

This chapter introduced you to the C programming language, along with different versions of C. You learned about the structure of C programs, coding guidelines, and keywords in C. Then you saw how to create, compile, and launch a simple C program.

You also learned about data types in C and C operators (such as arithmetic operators, increment/decrement operators, and ternary operators). You also learned about variables in C, indentation/code format, and assignment statements in C. Finally, you learned about arrays in C and how to add the numbers in an array.

CONDITIONAL LOGIC AND SIMPLE TASKS

This chapter is essentially a continuation of the material in Chapter 1, with code samples that use conditional logic in C programs, followed by examples of performing routine tasks in C. Please note that the code samples in this chapter provide an assortment of topics whose coverage is limited to basic functionality. At the same time, these code samples contain some "building blocks" for more interesting code samples in subsequent chapters.

The first part starts with examples of comments in C programs, followed by various examples of conditional logic for handling tasks such as checking if a given year is a leap year, finding the largest of three numbers, and calculating the third angle of a triangle. The second part of this chapter contains a code sample that shows the difference between local and global variables, followed by type casting and integer promotion in C programs.

The third section explains how to handle user input in C programs, using the C functions `gets()`, `puts()`, `scanf()`, and `printf()`. You will see how to read formatted and unformatted input values, and how to read an entire line of user input.

The final section briefly discusses `stdin`, `stdout`, and `stderr` that represent standard input, standard output, and standard error, respectively, that can be redirected to accept input from files (for standard input) and also redirected to output files (for standard output and standard error).

COMMENTS IN C PROGRAMS

Although the C programs in this book are very short and do not benefit much (if at all) from comments, remember that comments in your code can help other people understand your code (and perhaps also you, if you haven't looked at your code for quite some time). There are several ways to include comments in C programs, some of which are shown here:

```
/* this is a comment */
// this is a second comment
/* this is
a third comment */
```

The rule of thumb is simple: include a comment (or a comment block) to explain a section of code whose purpose might be difficult to understand. Obviously, you don't need to include a comment when the code is self-explanatory, such as the following:

```
int x = 3;      // an integer
float y = 4.5;  // a decimal
int *ptr;       // a pointer to an integer
return x;       // return the value of x
```

SIMPLE CONDITIONAL LOGIC

This section shows you a very simple example of using if-else statements in C programs. Make note of the examples of conditional logic in this chapter because (as you will see in Chapter 3) for loops in C programs invariably contain some type of conditional logic (with the possible exception of C programs that provide report-related functionality).

Listing 2.1 displays the contents of IfElse.c that illustrates how to use if-else logic in a C program.

LISTING 2.1: IfElse.c

```
#include <stdio.h>

int main()
{
    int z = 10;

    if(z % 2 == 0)
    {
        printf("z is even: %d\n", z);
    }
    else
    {
        printf("z is odd: %d\n", z);
    }

    return 0;
}
```

Listing 2.1 is straightforward: the variable z is initialized as an integer with the value of 10, followed by a conditional code block that prints one message if z is even, and a different message if z is odd. The output from compiling and launching the code in Listing 2.1 is here:

```
z is even: 10
```

CONDITIONAL LOGIC WITH LOGICAL ERRORS

Listing 2.2 displays the contents of `IfElse2.c` that illustrates how to use slightly more complicated `if-else` logic in a C program.

LISTING 2.2: IfElse2.c

```c
#include <stdio.h>

int main()
{
    int z=10, y=-123, w=0;

    w = (z/2)*2;
    if(z == w)
    {
        printf("z is even: %d\n", z);
    }
    else
    {
        printf("z is odd: %d\n", z);
    }

    if(z = y)  // do you mean == instead of =?
    {
        printf("z is even: %d\n", z);
    }
    else
    {
        printf("z is odd: %d\n", z);
    }

    return 0;
}
```

Listing 2.2 initializes the integer-valued variables z, y, and w, followed by an arithmetic expression that is an alternative to using the % operator to determine whether an integer is even. If you divide an integer by 2 and then multiply that number by 2, the result equals the initial integer *only* if it's even: this is true because division by 2 truncates the non-integer portion.

For example, 3 is odd because (3/2)*2 = 1*2 = 2, which does not equal 3, whereas 4 is even because (4/2)*2 = 2*2 = 4.

The next section of Listing 2.2 contains conditional logic that displays one message if z is even and a different message if z is odd. The second block of code contain conditional logic that involves a simple logic error: the use of "=" (which is an assignment operator) instead of "==" (which is a logical operator). Logical errors do not cause compilation errors: they produce results that are often incorrect, but more difficult to detect (although in this example the output shows the obvious error).

The output from compiling and launching the code in Listing 2.2 is here (the second line of output is not what you might expect):

```
z is even: 10
z is even: -123
```

The second line of output is due to the incorrect syntax in Listing 2.2 that involves a single "=" sign instead of two "==" signs. The code snippet **if(z = y)** is an assignment expression that evaluates to the value assigned, which is -123. Since -123 is *not* equal to 0, the if portion of the code is true. Consequently, the code inside the if portion is executed, which is why the following incorrect output is printed:

```
z is even: -123
```

Although this specific logical error can be easily discovered, logical errors can be much more difficult to detect, especially in long and complex C programs.

ARITHMETIC OPERATORS AND CONDITIONAL LOGIC

Listing 2.3 displays the contents of IfElse3.c that illustrates how to use multiple if-else code blocks in a C program. Recall the code sample in Chapter 1 that uses %d for formatting purposes in the printf() function.

LISTING 2.3: IfElse3.c

```c
#include <stdio.h>

int main()
{
    int x=8, y=-12, z=10;

    printf("x: %d y: %d z: %d\n",x,y,z);

    if( x == 3 ) { z = 0; }
    else         { z = 8; }
    printf("x: %d y: %d z: %d\n",x,y,z);

    if( y < 0 )  { z *= 3; }
    printf("x: %d y: %d z: %d\n",x,y,z);

    if(z % 2 == 0) { x /= 4; }
    else           { y *= -1; }
    printf("x: %d y: %d z: %d\n",x,y,z);

    return 0;
}
```

Listing 2.3 contains three code blocks involving conditional logic, after which there is a printf() statement that prints the result. The first code block updates the value of z based on the value of x. The second code block updates the value of z based on whether the value of y is less than 0. The third code block updates the value of x or y depending on whether the value of z is even or odd, respectively.

The output from compiling and launching the code in Listing 2.3 is here:

```
x:  8  y:  -12  z:  10
x:  8  y:  -12  z:  8
x:  8  y:  -12  z:  24
x:  2  y:  -12  z:  24
```

COMPOUND IF-ELSE STATEMENTS

C supports the operator && for testing whether two or more conditions are true (otherwise the result is false). C also supports the || operator that returns true if one condition (from a set of multiple conditions) is true, otherwise the result is false.

Listing 2.4 displays the contents of IfElse4.c that illustrates how to use compound if-else logic in a C program.

LISTING 2.4: IfElse4.c

```c
#include <stdio.h>

int main()
{
   int x=-8, z=10;

   if((z > 5) && (z < 15))
   {
      printf("z between 5 and 15: %d\n", z);
   }
   else
   {
      printf("z NOT between 5 and 15: %d\n", z);
   }

   if((x < 0) || (z > 4))
   {
      printf("x negative or z greater than 4: %d\n", z);
   }
   else
   {
      printf("x non-negative or z less than 4: %d\n", z);
   }

   return 0;
}
```

Listing 2.4 contains two code blocks involving conditional logic. The first code block checks whether the value of z is between 5 and 15: if true, then the corresponding message is printed (otherwise the appropriate message is printed). The second code block checks if x is negative or z is greater than 4: if either condition is true, then the appropriate message is displayed (and if not, the counter-factual statement in displayed).

The output from compiling and launching the code in Listing 2.4 is here:

```
z between 5 and 15: 10
x negative or z greater than 4: 10
```

What is "Short Circuiting"?

In general, if an expression contains multiple and statements, the result is false if *any* of the and statements is false, and therefore there is no need to check the remaining and terms (if any). This behavior is called "short circuiting," a simple example is shown here:

```c
int x = 3;
if( (x < 4 ) && (x > 5) && (x < 0))
{
    // do something
}
else
{
    // do something else
}
```

In the previous compound if expression, (x > 5) is false, so there is no need to evaluate the other portions of the if expression, and the else portion is executed.

Short circuiting occurs in other types of conditional logic. For example, if a compound if expression *succeeds* at an intermediate point, then the remaining portion of the compound if expression is not evaluated. Here is an example:

```c
int x = 3;
if (x > 5)
{
    // do something
}
else if (x < 4)
{
    // do something else
}
else if (x < 0)
{
    // do yet another thing
}
```

The preceding code block is true in the first else statement, so there is no need to check the remaining portion of the expression.

A third example of short circuiting is a combination of the previous two examples, as shown here:

```c
int x = 3, y = 7;
if (x > 5)
{
    // print something
}
else if (x < 4)
{
    if (y < 2)
    {
        // print something
```

```
      }
      else if (y < 4)
      {
         // print something else
      }
      else if (y < 6)
      {
         // print yet another thing
      }
   }
   else if (x < 0)
   {
      // do yet another thing
   }
```

The preceding code block is true in the first else statement, so the remaining portions of the compound if expression involving x are not executed. However, all the expressions involving y are false, which means that nothing is executed in the nested if expression involving the variable y. If necessary, read this example again until it's clear to you that nothing is printed.

RANKING NUMBERS WITH IF-ELSE STATEMENTS

Listing 2.5 displays the contents of OrderedValues.c that illustrates how to use if-else logic in a C program to display three numbers in descending order.

LISTING 2.5: OrderedValues.c

```c
#include <stdio.h>

int main()
{
   int a1=3, a2=8, a3=6, temp;

   printf("ORIGINAL a1: %d a2: %d a3: %d\n", a1, a2, a3);

   if( a1 < a2 )
   {
      temp = a1;
      a1 = a2;
      a2 = temp;
   }

   if( a2 < a3 )
   {
      temp = a2;
      a2 = a3;
      a3 = temp;
   }

   printf("ORDERED  a1: %d a2: %d a3: %d\n", a1, a2, a3);
```

```
    return 0;
}
```

Listing 2.5 initializes the variables a1, a2, and a3, and prints their initial values. The first code block swaps the values of a1 and a2 only if a1 is less than a2. Similarly, the second code block swaps the values of a2 and a3 only if the value of a2 is less than a3. The output from compiling and launching the code in Listing 2.5 is here:

```
ORIGINAL a1: 3 a2: 8 a3: 6
ORDERED  a1: 8 a2: 6 a3: 3
```

SEQUENTIAL IF STATEMENTS

Listing 2.6 displays the contents of MaxAndMin.c that illustrates how to use if-else logic in a C program in order to find the maximum value and the minimum value of three numbers.

LISTING 2.6: MaxAndMin.c

```
#include <stdio.h>

int main()
{
    int a1=3, a2=8, a3=6,max=0, min=0;
    max = a1;
    min = a1;

    if( max < a2 ) { max = a2; }
    if( min > a2 ) { min = a2; }

    if( max < a3 ) { max = a3; }
    if( min > a3 ) { min = a3; }

    printf("ORIGINAL a1: %d a2: %d a3: %d\n", a1, a2, a3);
    printf("MAXIMUM: %d\n", max);
    printf("MINIMUM: %d\n", min);

    return 0;
}
```

Listing 2.6 starts by setting the value of max and the value of min equal to a1. The next pair of statements compares the value of max and min with the value of a2, and updates them accordingly. Similarly, the second code block compares the value of max and min with the value of a3, and updates them accordingly.

The output from compiling and launching the code in Listing 2.6 is here:

```
ORIGINAL a1: 3 a2: 8 a3: 6
MAXIMUM: 8
MINIMUM: 3
```

NESTED IF-ELSE STATEMENTS

Listing 2.7 displays the contents of AngleSum.c that illustrates how to use if-else logic in a C program to determine the third angle of a triangle, based on the value of the first two angles. Keep in mind that all angles must be greater than 0 and less than 180, and that the sum of a pair of angles must be less than 180.

LISTING 2.7: AngleSum.c

```
#include <stdio.h>

int main()
{
    int a1=40, a2=80, a3=0;
    // ensure the following are true:
    // 1) a1>0 and a1 < 180
    // 2) a2>0 and a2 < 180
    // 3) a1+a1 < 180

    if( ((a1 <= 0) || (a1 >= 180))  ||
        ((a2 <= 0) || (a2 >= 180)) )
    {
        printf("angles out of range: a1 = %d a2 = %d\n", a1,
a2);
    }
    else
    {
        if( a1+a2 >= 180)
        {
            printf("a1 + a2 is too large: %d\n", a1+a2);
        }
        else
        {
            a3 = 180 - (a1+a2);
            printf("a1: %d a2: %d a3: %d\n", a1, a2, a3);
        }
    }

    return 0;
}
```

Listing 2.7 first ensures that a1 and a2 are both between 0 and 180 degrees. If this test succeeds, the next portion of code checks if a1+a2 is at least 180: if so, the values are too large to form a triangle. Otherwise, the value of a3 is set equal to 180-(a1+a2), and the appropriate message is displayed.

This concludes the portion of the chapter involving conditional logic. In Chapter 1 you learned about the scope of variables, and the next several sections contain examples of variables having different scopes in C programs.

SCOPE OF VARIABLES IN C

The scope of a variable is a region of the program where a defined variable can be accessed. There are three types of variable scope in C programs:

- Inside a function definition or code block (local variables)
- Outside of any function definition (global variables)
- As a parameter in a function definition (formal parameters)

If a variable with the same name is defined globally and also as a formal parameter or inside a function definition, then the global variable has lower priority. Note that a variable cannot be defined twice, either globally or locally, which means that they must be defined in different scopes.

Global Variables in C Programs

The rule regarding global variables is simple: avoid them as much as possible. One reason for the popularity of OOP (Object Oriented Programming) languages is the concept of encapsulation: variables are kept in the classes where they belong. The value of a variable is accessed and modified via "getters" and "setters" (also called "accessors" and "mutators").

Although OOP languages do not remove the need for global variables in all cases, they enable you to vastly reduce the number of global variables in an application. Later in this chapter you will see code samples with global variables in C.

GLOBAL VERSUS LOCAL VARIABLES

Local variables are declared inside a function or a code block, and they are only accessible inside the function or block of code where they are declared. Hence, local variables are unavailable to other functions or blocks of code that are outside the block where they are defined. In other words, the values of local variables are "lost" when the function returns to the caller.

On the other hand, global variables are defined outside of functions, often in the initial portion of a C program. Global variables retain their value throughout the lifetime of a C program (i.e., until the program exits).

Listing 2.8 displays the contents of `LocalVars.c` that illustrates how to define local variables.

LISTING 2.8: LocalVars.c

```c
#include <stdio.h>

// global variable declaration
int a=1, b=2, c=3;

void printGlobalVariables()
{
```

```
   printf ("Inside the printGlobalVariables function\n");
   printf ("GLOBAL value of a = %d, b = %d and c =
%d\n",a,b,c);
}

int main()
{
   printf ("GLOBAL value of a = %d, b = %d and c =
%d\n",a,b,c);

   // local variable declaration
   int a, b, c;

   // actual initialization
   a = 10;
   b = 20;
   c = a + b;

   printf ("LOCAL value of a = %d, b = %d and c =
%d\n",a,b,c);

   printGlobalVariables();

   return 0;
}
```

Listing 2.8 is very simple: the integer-valued *global* variables a, b, and c are declared and initialized, after which their values are printed immediately inside the main() function. The next portion of code inside the main() function declares and initializes *local* integer-valued variables a, b, and c and then prints their values. The final portion of the main() function invokes the print-GlobalVariables() function that simply prints the values of the *global* integer-valued variables a, b, and c.

The output from Listing 2.8 is here:

```
GLOBAL value of a = 1, b = 2 and c = 3
LOCAL value of a = 10, b = 20 and c = 30
Inside the printGlobalVariables function
GLOBAL value of a = 1, b = 2 and c = 3
```

Recall that if a variable of the same name is defined globally and locally, the value of the local variable has priority over the global variable when a function (containing that local variable) is executed. Outside of a function, the opposite is true (which must be the case because a locally defined variable is not accessible outside the function where it is defined).

TYPE CASTING IN C

Type casting allows you to convert the data type of a variable to a different data type. For example, the sum of a set of integers is an integer, but the average value is usually a double instead of an integer.

Since every `long` data type can represent any `int` value without losing any precision, an `int` value can automatically be converted to a value of type `long`. However, if you want to treat a `long` as an `int`, there can be a loss of precision. Similarly, if you cast a `double` value as an `int` value, there will be loss of precision.

Convert values from one type to another via the cast operator as follows:

```
(type_name) expression
```

Listing 2.9 displays the contents of `TypeCast.c` that illustrates the difference between an average that is calculated as an `int` data type and an average that is calculated as a `double` data type.

LISTING 2.9: TypeCast.c

```c
#include <stdio.h>

int main()
{
    int x1=11, x2=4, x3=0;
    double x4;

    x3 = x1/x2;
    x4 = (double) x1/x2;

    printf("x1: %d\n",x1);
    printf("x2: %d\n",x2);
    printf("x3: %d\n",x3);
    printf("x4: %f\n",x4);

    return 0;
}
```

Listing 2.9 initializes the integer-valued variables `x1`, `x2`, and `x3`. The next code block updates `x3`, and then initializes the value of `x4`.

The output from compiling and executing the code in Listing 2.9 is here:

```
x1: 11
x2: 4
x3: 2
x4: 2.750000
```

NOTE *The cast operator has precedence over division.*

The value of `sum` is converted to type `double`, after which it is divided by `count`, which in turn results in a `double` value. Type conversions can be implicit (and performed by the compiler automatically), or they can be made explicitly using the cast operator.

Integer Promotion

Integer promotion is the process by which values of integer type "smaller" than `int` or `unsigned int` are converted either to `int` or `unsigned int`.

Listing 2.10 displays the contents of `PromoteVar.c` that illustrates the result of adding a character to a variable that has an `int` data type.

LISTING 2.10: PromoteVar.c

```
#include <stdio.h>

int main()
{
    int x1=11, x2=4, x3=0;
    double x4;

    x3 = x1/x2;
    x4 = (double) x1/x2;

    printf("x1: %d\n",x1);
    printf("x2: %d\n",x2);
    printf("x3: %d\n",x3);
    printf("x4: %f\n",x4);

    return 0;
}
```

Listing 2.10 initializes the integer-valued variables $x1$, $x2$, and $x3$. The next code block updates $x3$, and then initializes the value of $x4$. The final code block displays the double-based values for $x1$, $x2$, and $x3$, followed by the decimal value of f.

Listing 2.10 initializes the integer-valued variables $x1$, $x2$, and $x3$. The next code block updates $x3$, and then initializes the value of $x4$. The output from compiling and executing the code in Listing 2.10 is here:

```
x:   10
c:   65
s1: 75
s2: K
```

The next section discusses two useful built-in functions that enable you to make a copy of a string. In Chapter 4, you will see a list of other useful built-in functions in C.

THE STRCPY() AND STRNCPY() FUNCTIONS IN C

The `strcpy(string1, string2)` function copies `string2`, including the ending null character, to the location that is specified by `string1` (notice that this is a right-to-left operation) The `strcpy()` function operates on null-terminated strings. The string arguments to the `strcpy()` function should contain a null character (`\0`) that marks the end of the string because no length checking is performed. Avoid using a literal string for `string1`, but `string2` can be a literal string.

Listing 2.11 displays the contents of CopyFunction.c that illustrates how to use the strncpy() function.

LISTING 2.11: CopyFunction.c

```
#include <stdio.h>
#include <string.h>

#define BUFFER_SIZE 80

int main()
{
  char source[BUFFER_SIZE] = "The initial string";
  char destination[BUFFER_SIZE] = "The target string";
  char *result;

  printf("Before: %s\n", destination);
  result = strcpy(destination, source);
  printf("After:  %s\n", destination);

  return 0;
}
```

Listing 2.11 uses the #define preprocessor (discussed in more detail in Chapter 7) to set BUFFER_SIZE equal to 10. Next, a main() function initializes the character arrays source and destination to hard-coded strings. A printf() statement displays the contents of destination, followed by an invocation of the strcpy() method that copies the contents of source to the variable destination, after which another printf() statement displays the new contents of destination. The output from launching Listing 2.11 is here:

```
Before: The target string
After:  The initial string
```

STRINGS AND STRING-RELATED FUNCTIONS

A string in C consists of a sequence of characters. Unlike languages such as Java, C does not provide a built-in string type. C uses a character array to represent a string, which is always terminated with '\0'.

Listing 2.12 displays the contents of CharArray.c that illustrates how to initialize an array of characters.

LISTING 2.12: CharArray.c

```
#include <stdio.h>

char name[4];

int main()
{
    name[0] = 'a';
    name= 'b';
```

```
    name= 'c';
    name= '\0';

    return (0);
}
```

Listing 2.12 declares a character array name that contains 4 elements (currently uninitialized). Next, a main() function initializes each element of the name array with the characters "a", "b", and "c". The final position is null-terminated with '\0'.

The strcpy() Function

String constants consist of text enclosed in double quotes (""), as shown here:

```
char str[] = "abcd";
```

Although other languages (such as Java) allow you to assign one string to another string, the following statement is illegal in C:

```
str = "another string"; // illegal in C
```

As you saw in an previous code sample, C provides the built-in strcpy() function to copy a string into a another location. Listing 2.13 displays the contents of CopyString.c that illustrates how to use the strcpy() function.

LISTING 2.13: CopyString.c

```
#include <string.h>

char str[4];

int main()
{
    strcpy(str, "abc");

    return (0);
}
```

Listing 2.13 is minimalistic: after declaring the character string str that consists of 4 elements, the main() function copies the string "abc" into the variable str.

In addition, you can specify variable-length strings. As an example, Listing 2.14 displays the contents of Array50.c that illustrates how to define a variable that can contain up to 50 characters.

Listing 2.14: Array50.c

```
#include <string.h>
#include <stdio.h>
```

```c
char name[50];

int main()
{
    strcpy(name, "abcd"); // Initialize the name
    printf("The name is %s\n", name);

    return (0);
}
```

Listing 2.14 declares a character variable `name` of length 50, followed by the `main()` function that invokes the `strcpy()` command to copy the string `abcd` to the variable `name`.

Although the size of the `name` array is 50, the length of the string `abcd` in the preceding code block is 4. You can copy any string up to 49 characters in length to the variable `name`: one position (typically the rightmost one) is reserved for `'\0'` that indicates end-of-string. The dimension of the string variable is 50 because we *assume* that all names are at most 49 characters in length.

However, if you attempt to assign a string whose length is greater than 49 to the name variable, this copy operation requires memory that is not assigned to the enclosing program. As a result, the program will perform unexpectedly, or provide incorrect results, or even crash.

Listing 2.15 displays the contents of `Strcpy1.c` that illustrates how to use the `strcpy()` function to initialize three character arrays.

LISTING 2.15: Strcpy1.c

```c
#include <stdio.h>
#include <string.h>

char first[100];
char last[100];
char fullName[200];

int main()
{
    strcpy(first, "John");
    strcpy(last, "Smith");
    strcpy(fullName, first);

    strcat(fullName, " ");
    strcat(fullName, last);
    printf("The full name is %s\n", fullName);

    return 0;
}
```

Listing 2.15 declares the character variables `first`, `last`, and `fullName` of lengths 100, 100, and 200, respectively.

Next, the `main()` function invokes the `strcpy()` function to copy the strings `John`, `Smith`, and the variable `first` into the variables `first`, `last`, and `fullName`, respectively.

The final portion of code invokes the `strcat()` function to concatenate the variable `fullName` with a space (" ") and the second invocation of the `strcat()` function appends the value of last to the variable `fullName`. The final `printf()` statement displays the value of the variable `fullName`. The output of this program is:

```
The full name is John Smith
```

HANDLING USER INPUT IN C

There are three pairs of built-in C functions for reading user input and then printing the result. The three input functions read a character, a single line, and a single line with a specified format. The first input function is `getchar()` that reads a single character from standard input (and returns an `int`).

The second input function is `gets()` that returns a character pointer. The use of this method is deferred until you learn about C pointers (Chapter 5 and Chapter 6). The third input function is `scanf()` that reads input from the standard input stream and scans that input according to format provided. The `scanf()` function also involves a pointer (so it will be deferred until after the discussion about pointers).

The `getchar()` & `putchar()` Functions: Single Character Functions

The standard does not specify whether getchar() and putchar() are macros. However, the reason that their return value is an `int` (not a `char` value) is because they are stream-oriented and can interact with files. The point is important if you want to follow safe coding practices.

Keyboard input provides `char` values, but file input can generate `int` values, such as the EOF or End of File value, which is an `int`. And file output can generate `int` values on file errors. Safe coding practices dictate that you consider these conditions.

The `getchar(void)` function is straightforward: it reads the next available character (supplied by user input or redirected from a file) and returns that character as an integer (this function has a return type of `int`). Since this function reads a single character, you can place this function inside a loop if you need to read multiple input characters.

On the other hand, the `putchar(int c)` function renders a single character as its output. Since this function also renders one character, you can place this function inside a loop if you need to render multiple characters. You will see examples of both these functions later in the chapter.

The `scanf()` and `printf()` Functions: Multiple Characters

The `scanf(const char *format, ...)` function can read multiple characters from the standard input stream. This function specifies a format, so the input is scanned based on the format that is specified.

In fact, the `scanf()` function returns the number of variables that it filled with data, and we can inspect this value by setting some variable of type int equal to this number, as shown here:

```
int numfilled;
numfilled = scanf(" %d , %d",&number1,&number2);
```

Next, inspect the value of `numfilled` to determine how many of the variables were populated with data.

The `printf()` function has the form `printf(const char *format,...)`, and as you saw in Chapter 1, this function writes output to the standard output stream according to the format that is specified in the specific invocation. For example, Listing 2.16 displays the contents of `PrintfSamples.c` that illustrates the use of the `printf()` function with various data types and formats.

LISTING 2.16: PrintfSamples.c

```
#include <stdio.h>

int main()
{
    int x1 = 23;
    double x2 = 1234.56789;

    printf("Hello World\n");
    printf("%s\n", "Hello World");
    printf("%d\n", 17);
    printf("%s %d %5.2f\n", "Hello World", x1, x2);

    return 0;
}
```

Listing 2.16 contains a `main()` function that initializes the variable `x1` with 23 and the variable `x2` with `1234.56789`. The next section consists of four `printf()` statements that display various numbers and strings.

The format of the values that are displayed via the `printf()` function can be a simple constant string, but you can specify %s, %d, %c, %f, and so forth, in order to print or read strings, integer, character, or float respectively. There are many other formatting options available that you can use, based on your requirements. The output from Listing 2.13 is here:

```
Hello World
Hello World
17
Hello World 23 1234.57
```

Now that you understand the purpose of the input-related functions in this section, let's delve into some code samples that obtain user input from the command line.

C11 COMPLIANCE

The C11 standard introduced new functions that are secure alternatives to their predecessors. These functions have "_s" (for "secure") appended to their name. For example, the functions strtok_s, strcat_s, and strcpy_s are replaced with strtok_s, strcat_s, and strcpy_s, respectively.

The new functions are safe because they have an extra size parameter that limits the string operations. The size parameter prevents a missing null terminator from overrunning the end of a buffer. However, support for bounds-checking functions is optional, and they are only available in implementations that define the macro __STD_LIB_EXT1__. If the new functions are available, they are included in the standard "header" files, along with their older counterparts. In order to "tell" the compiler to provide these new functions, you need to define a macro before the relevant header file, an example of which is here:

```
#define __STDC_WANT_LIB_EXT1__ 1
#include <stdio.h>
```

Keep in mind that if you do not define the preceding macro before the relevant header file, the visibility of the secure functions depends on your particular compiler. In addition, if you want to ensure that secure functions are not visible, set the preceding macro to 0 instead of 1.

In addition to the new bound-checking safe functions in C11, you also need to use the fgets() function instead of the gets() function. Avoid the latter function because you cannot determine how many characters this function will read (unless you know in advance). Since you cannot predict how much "room" or space in memory the gets() will require in order to store the string inputted by users, there is a chance that the string will corrupt memory that does not belong to the currently executing C program. Hence, gets() cannot be used safely in every situation. Later in this chapter you will see examples of the behavior of the fgets() function and the gets() function.

The ANSI/ISO committee for C11 also sought to standardize well-known working paradigms and features that already exist in the majority of big compilers (and not to implement new features). The N1570 draft of the C11 standard is here:

http://www.open-std.org/jtc1/sc22/wg14/www/docs/n1570.pdf

The document that describes the changes from C99 to C11 is here:

https://en.wikipedia.org/wiki/C11_(C_standard_revision)#Changes_from_C99

At this point there don't seem to be any fully C11-compliant compiler implementations.

In addition to the new safe functions, C11 provides additions to the C language, some of which are:

- Unicode support
- floating point support for IEC 60559 (optional)

- multi-threading support (optional)
- anonymous structs and unions
- the `alignas` and `alignof` keywords
- bounds checking functions (string library)

Perform an online search to obtain more information about the items in this list.

Checking for C11 Compliance

The first (and simplest) way to check for C11 compliance involves specifying the switch `-std=c11` whenever you compile a C program, an example of which is shown here:

```
gcc -std=c11 HelloWorld.c -o HelloWorld
```

However, you will *not* see a non-compliance warning message until you launch the executable (i.e., the compilation step does not generate non-compliance messages), as shown later in this section.

Second, replace the `gets` function, deprecated in the previous C language standard revision, ISO/IEC 9899:1999/Cor.3:2007(E), with a new safe alternative called `gets_s` if it's available, or use the `fgets` function.

As a simple illustration, here is a code sample called `SafeStrcpy1.c` that attempts to use the `strcpy_s` function:

```
#define __STDC_WANT_LIB_EXT1__ 1
#include <stdio.h>
#include <string.h>

char first[100];

int main()
{
    strcpy_s(first, "John");
    return 0;
}
```

Here is the output during the compilation of SafeStrcpy1.c:

```
SafeStrcpy1.c: In function 'main':
SafeStrcpy1.c:9:4: warning: implicit declaration of
function 'strcpy_s'; did you mean 'strcpy'? [-Wimplicit-
function-declaration]
    strcpy_s(first, "John");
    ^~~~~~~~
    strcpy
Undefined symbols for architecture x86_64:
  "_strcpy_s", referenced from:
      _main in cck31S8F.o
ld: symbol(s) not found for architecture x86_64
collect2: error: ld returned 1 exit status
```

The preceding code is on a Macbook Pro with MacOS Sierra (version 10.12.6), and here is the information about `gcc` that was used in the compilation step:

```
$ gcc --version
gcc (MacPorts gcc7 7.2.0_0) 7.2.0
Copyright (C) 2017 Free Software Foundation, Inc.
```

What about C17 Compliance?

There are no new features included in C17. However, C17 will include all accepted C11 defect reports, but no new features. According to GCC reference, C17 is a bug-fix version of the C11 standard with DR (Defect Report) resolutions integrated. C17 provides the switch -std=c17 (the counterpart to -std=c11 for C11), as well as -std=gnu17 (instead of -std=gnu11).

In case you're interested, the C17 report is available for purchase here (USD 116):

https://webstore.ansi.org/RecordDetail.aspx?sku=INCITS%2fISO%2fIEC +9899%3a2011+(R2017)

THE `FGETS ()` FUNCTION (C11 COMPLIANT)

This section contains a code sample that shows you how the behavior of the fgets() function differs from the gets() function (discussed in the next section). Whether or not you read the code samples, make sure you remember to use the fgets() function and *never* use the gets() function.

Listing 2.17 displays the contents of the C program testfgets1.c that illustrates the use of the fgets() function.

LISTING 2.17: testfgets.c

```c
#include <stdio.h>
#define MAX 10

int main()
{
    char buf[MAX];
    fgets(buf, MAX, stdin);
    printf("string is: %s\n", buf);

    return 0;
}
```

The code is very simple: users are prompted to enter a string and that string is re-displayed at the command prompt. Now compile the code in Listing 2.17 as follows:

```
gcc -std=c11 testfgets.c -o testfgets
```

Launch the executable and enter a string:

```
$ ./testfgets
this is a long string and let's see what happens
string is: this is a
```

Keep in mind that Listing 2.17 allows for 8 characters of input, the '\0' terminator, and the end-of-line '\n' character (which is considered part of the input string). On the other hand, the gets function only appends '\0' (but not the '\n' character).

However, what if users press <RETURN> after entering more than 10 characters? In this scenario, the final carriage return is not read by fgets, which means that we need to check that there is a carriage return that was read in the first 9 characters; if it's not present, then we need to shift the '\0' to the right one position.

THE GETS() FUNCTION (NOT C11 COMPLIANT)

Listing 2.18 displays the contents of the C program testgets1.c that illustrates the use of the gets() function.

LISTING 2.18: testgets.c

```
#include <stdio.h>
#define MAX 10

int main()
{
    char buf[MAX];

    printf("Enter a string: ");
    gets(buf);
    printf("string is: %s\n", buf);
}
```

The code is very simple: users a prompted to enter a string and that string is re-displayed at the command prompt. Now compile the code in Listing 2.18 as follows:

```
gcc -std=c11 testgets.c -o testgets
```

Launch the executable and enter a string:

```
$ ./testgets
warning: this program uses gets(), which is unsafe.
Enter a string: this is a long string and let's see what
happens
string is: this is a long string and let's see what happens
Segmentation fault: 11
```

NOTE   *The unsafe message is displayed only when you launch the executable and not during the compilation/link step.*

There is one significant impediment to using the safe string functions: although safe functions (such as strcpy_s and strtok_s others) are specified by the C standard since C11, they are actually optional in C11 because all standard library implementations are not required to provide optional features. Hence, in order to get `strcpy_s` and `strtok_s` and all the other safe string functions into your system, you will need to either 1) find a library that implements them all, or 2) implement them yourself.

Finally, the following websites allow you to copy/paste code snippets into their Web pages in order to check for C11 compliance:

https://godbolt.org/
https://wandbox.org/

READING A SINGLE CHARACTER FROM THE COMMAND LINE

Listing 2.19 displays the contents of `ReadSingleChar.c` that illustrates how to use the `getchar()` function to read a single character from standard input and then print that character using the `putchar()` function in a C program.

LISTING 2.19: ReadSingleChar.c

```
#include <stdio.h>

int main()
{
    int c;

    printf( "Enter a value :");
    c = getchar();

    printf( "\nYou entered: ");
    putchar( c );

    return 0;
}
```

Listing 2.19 contains a `main()` function that declares the integer variable c, followed by a `printf()` statement that prompts users for input. After users press a key on the keyboard, the built-in `getchar()` C function assigns that value to the variable c. The next portion of code displays the value that users entered at the keyboard. A sample invocation of launching the code in Listing 2.19 is here:

```
Enter a value :f

You entered: f
```

READING AN UNFORMATTED LINE FROM THE COMMAND LINE

Listing 2.20 displays the contents of `ReadLine.c` that illustrates how to read a line of text from the keyboard and displays its length.

LISTING 2.20: ReadLine.c

```c
#include <string.h>
#include <stdio.h>

char line[100];

int main()
{
  printf("Enter a line: ");
  fgets(line, sizeof(line), stdin);
  printf("The length of the line is: %d\n", strlen(line));

  return (0);
}
```

Listing 2.20 declares a character variable line of length 100, followed by a
main() function with a printf() statement that prompts users for input. This
time users can enter more than one character (i.e., a complete sentence whose
length is at most 99). After users provide their input, the built-in fgets() C
function assigns that input to the variable line. The next portion of code displays the input string that users entered at the keyboard. A sample invocation
of launching the code in Listing 2.20 is here:

```
Enter a line: this is a simple input line
The length of the line is: 28
```
**Another invocation of launching the code in Listing 2.20 is
here:**
```
Enter a line: abcd
The length of the line is: 5
```

Notice that the string abcd is only four characters: where does the extra character come from? The function fgets() also includes the end-of-line '\n' in
the string (i.e., the fifth character).

The sizeof() function also provides a convenient way of limiting the
number of characters read to the maximum numbers that the variable can
hold.

Here's an interesting question: given an array myarr of an unknown primitive data type and unknown length, how can you determine the number of
items in the array?

The simple (elegant?) answer involves the sizeof() operator, as shown
here:

```c
// myarr is defined elsewhere
int len = sizeof(myarr)/sizeof(myarr[0]);
```

Since the elements of the array myarr have the same data type, they all have
the same size, which means that the length of the array myarr is a multiple of
the size of the first (or any other) element in the array. This operator will be
discussed in more detail in Chapter 6.

READING A FORMATTED LINE FROM THE COMMAND LINE

Listing 2.21 displays the contents of ReadFormattedLine.c that illustrates how to read a formatted line from standard input via the scanf() function in a C program.

LISTING 2.21: ReadFormattedLine.c

```
#include <stdio.h>

int main( )
{
   char str[100];
   int i, numfilled;

   printf( "Enter a string and an int :");
   numfilled = scanf("%s %d", str, &i);

   printf("\nNumber of filled values: %d\n",numfilled);
   printf("\nYou entered values for the string and the
int");
   printf("\nYou entered the string %s and the number %d ",
str, i);

   return 0;
}
```

Listing 2.29 contains a main() function that declares a character variable line of length 100 and also declares an integer-valued variable i. Next, a printf() statement prompts users for input. This time users can enter a string and an integer, after which the built-in scanf() C function assigns the input string to str and the input integer to i.

There are two points to keep in mind. First, if you enter a string and press the <RETURN> key, the program seems to "hang" as it waits for you to enter a number. Second, any additional input beyond the number that you enter is ignored (see examples below).

After users provide their input, the printf() function displays the values of both of these variables. A sample invocation of launching the code in Listing 2.21 is here:

```
Enter a string and an int: abc 3

Number of filled values: 2

You entered values for the string and the int
You entered the string abc and the number 3
```

Another sample invocation of launching the code in Listing 2.21 is here:

```
Enter a string and an int: abc 3 4 5
```

```
Number of filled values: 2

You entered values for the string and the int
You entered the string abc and the number 3
```

THE BEHAVIOR OF THE SCANF() FUNCTION (OPTIONAL)

The behavior of the `scanf()` function in Listing 2.21 depends on the type of input that is provided. Specifically, if the provided input does not match the format string, the variables are never initialized. The C specification is very clear: as soon as there is a character from the input that does not match the "current part" of the format string that the `scanf()` function is trying to match, the matching process stops *immediately* without reading any more characters or assigning values to any more variables. In addition, anything that happens after the failure of the matching process is "undefined behavior."

For example, consider what happens when users provide the following input values after launching the code in Listing 2.21:

```
Enter a string and an int: abc x y z

Number of filled values: 1

You entered values for the string and the int
You entered the string abc and the number 1
```

Obviously, there is a mismatch between the input value x and the reported value 1, which is entirely unrelated. How do you detect this scenario? One approach is to assign known values to the variables before calling `scanf()`. If the variable has a known value, and then in the process of failing `scanf()` sets it to 1, that would be a severe bug in the implementation of `scanf()`, which is highly unlikely.

Trying to reason about "undefined behavior" is essentially a waste of time because absolutely *anything* can happen. However, here's a synopsis of what might be happening if you want some sort of intuitive understanding. Since the variable i (in the previous invocation) has not been initialized yet, then from the point of view of the compiler, its "lifetime" has not begun. The variable shares a register with some other variable whose lifetime ends before the variable is initialized. The other variable happens to get the value 1 under some conditions, and since the variable is uninitialized, it simply gets whatever was left over in the register. Hence, *uninitialized variables must never be read*: the compiler is allowed to assume that variables are never read before they are initialized and it can and does make optimizations based on those assumptions.

Note that not only does undefined behavior have no meaning, it can occur as soon as a compiler might be able to determine that it is inevitable. The way the code in Listing 2.21 is written, as soon as the `scanf()` function finishes with a less than complete result you have "undefined behavior."

In the case of the example at the beginning of this section, the "do absolutely anything" happens to be "on occasion under some specific circumstances, set the value of the variable i to 1." This is not a compiler bug because, by definition, once you have "undefined behavior" there is no such thing as a compiler bug. At that point there are no requirements on what code the compiler generates.

There are some additional interesting scenarios when you want to read strings and numbers from the command line, some of which are described here:

https://stackoverflow.com/questions/20867382/c-programming-scanf-not-working-correctly

READING MULTIPLE STRINGS FROM THE COMMAND LINE

Listing 2.22 displays the contents of `FirstLastName.c` that illustrates how to prompt users to enter the first name and the last name of a person.

LISTING 2.22: FirstLastName.c

```
#include <stdio.h>
#include <string.h>

char first[100];
char last[100];
char full[200];

int main()
{
    printf("Enter first name: ");
    fgets(first, sizeof(first), stdin);

    // see comment below about this snippet:
    // first[strlen(first)-1] = '\0';

    printf("Enter last name: ");
    fgets(last, sizeof(last), stdin);

    strcpy(full, first);
    strcat(full, " ");
    strcat(full, last);

    printf("The name is %s\n", full);

    return (0);
}
```

Listing 2.22 declares the character variables first, last, and fullName of lengths 100, 100, and 200, respectively. Next, the main() function uses 2 different printf() statements that prompts users for a first name and last name, using the built-in gets() C function to capture those input values.

The next part of the code uses the built-in `strcpy()` C function to copy first to the variable `full`. Next, the built-in `strcat()` function appends a space (" "), and then appends last to the variable `full`. A sample invocation of launching the code in Listing 2.22 is here:

```
Enter first name: john
Enter last name: smith
The name is john
 smith
```

Notice that the full name is displayed on separate lines, which happens because users must press a <RETURN> after entering the first name, and the <RETURN> character is included in the variable `full`. We can remove the <RETURN> character simply by uncommenting the following code snippet:

```
first[strlen(first)-1] = '\0';
```

However, enabling the preceding code snippet can produce undefined behavior if the variable `first` is an empty string, which could happen if this program receives an empty file as input. This aspect of the code in Listing 2.22 illustrates how easily you can inadvertently introduce a bug in your code. The solution is straightforward: *test the value of* `strlen(first)` *to ensure it is not 0 before truncating the string in the variable* `first` *via the preceding code snippet.*

Recompile the modified code and relaunch at the command line, and here is a sample invocation:

```
Enter first name: john
Enter last name: smith
The name is john smith
```

One more point to keep in mind: the preceding code snippet that removes the <RETURN> character results in undefined behavior if the variable `first` is an empty string. Hence, you need to modify the code in Listing 2.22 to test the value of `strlen(first)` to ensure that it is not 0 before you truncate the string.

USER INPUT FOR NUMERIC CALCULATIONS

Listing 2.23 displays the contents of `SimpleAdder.c` that illustrates how to prompt users for input, and then retrieve the input with the `fgets()` and `sscanf()` functions, all of which occurs inside a `while` loop.

LISTING 2.23: SimpleAdder.c

```
#include <stdio.h>

char line[100];  // line of data from the input
int result;      // the result of the calculations
char operator;   // operator the user specified
int value;       // value specified after the operator
```

```c
int main()
{
    result = 0; // initialize the final result

    while (1) {
        printf("Result: %d\n", result);
        printf("Enter operator and number: ");

        fgets(line, sizeof(line), stdin);
        sscanf(line, "%c %d", &operator, &value);

        if (operator == '+') { // why does "=" also work?
            result += value;
        }
        else if (operator == '-') {
            result -= value;
        }

        else {
            printf("Exiting loop: unknown operator: %c\n",
                        operator);
            break;
        }
    }

    return 0;
}
```

Listing 2.23 starts by initializing the variable result to 0. The main body of the program is a while loop that repeats until a break statement is reached. The body of the while loop contains a code block that prompts users for an operator and a number, as shown here:

```c
printf("Enter operator and number: ");
fgets(line, sizeof(line), stdin);
sscanf(line,"%c %d", &operator, &value);
```

These values are scanned and stored in the variables operator and value. The next portion of Listing 2.23 contains conditional logic that adds the two values if the operator is a plus sign (+); otherwise, an appropriate message is displayed.

A sample invocation of the code in Listing 2.23 is here:

```
Current Sum: 0
Enter operator and number: + 8
Current Sum: 8
Enter operator and number: - 4
Current Sum: 4
Enter operator and number: - 12
Current Sum: -8
Enter operator and number: + 100
Current Sum: 92
Enter operator and number:
```

```
Exiting loop: Unknown operator:

Final Sum: 92
```

Modify the code in Listing 2.21 to handle the cases where `operator` is `'*'` or `'/'`, which correspond to multiply and divide, and make sure that you handle division by zero correctly.

STDIN, STDOUT, AND STDERR

The C programming language treats devices as files. In addition, the following files are automatically opened when a C program executes:

- Standard File (File Pointer): Device
- Standard input (`stdin`): Keyboard
- Standard output (`stdout`): Screen
- Standard error (`stderr`): your screen

If you want a program to take its input from a file instead of the command line, you can do so by redirecting standard input, as shown here:

```
mybinaryfile <inputfile
```

You can redirect standard output and standard error to different files. For example, suppose you want to redirect standard output to the file `out1` and standard error to `bad1`. Use the following syntax:

```
mybinaryfile 1>out1 2>bad1
```

If you want to redirect standard output and standard error to the same file called `both1`, use the following syntax:

```
mybinaryfile 2>&1 1>both1
```

Other types of manipulation with file descriptors are possible. For example, you can close a file descriptor and open a new file descriptor. However, this topic is beyond the scope of this chapter.

SUMMARY

This chapter discussed local and global variables, followed by type casting and integer promotion. Next you learned about handling user input in C programs, along with the `gets()`, `puts()`, `scanf()`, and `printf()` functions.

You also learned about copying text strings via the `strcpy()` and `strncpy()` functions in C. Next you learned how to prompt users for single-character input via the `fgets()` function as well as formatted input using the `scanf()` function.

## CHAPTER 3

LOOPS AND ARRAYS

T his chapter contains code samples that illustrate how to use simple loops, nested loops, and arrays in C. The code samples perform string-related tasks, as well as an assortment of tasks with arrays of numbers and strings. In addition, many code samples contain if/else conditional logic that was introduced in Chapter 2 (please read that chapter if you have not already done so).

The first part of this chapter discusses basic loops, single-dimension and multi-dimensional arrays, and how to perform a linear search in arrays. The second part of this chapter calculates the maximum and minimum in an array of numbers, how to insert an element in an array, and how to delete an element from an array.

The third part of this chapter contains while loops, do-while loops, and string-related example involving while loops. Code samples in this section also contain conditional logic, which was introduced in Chapter 2. The final section contains code samples that determine the divisors of a positive integer and how to check if a number is prime.

WORKING WITH FOR LOOPS

Listing 3.1 displays the contents of ForLoop.c that shows you how to use a for loop in C.

LISTING 3.1: ForLoop.c

```c
#include <stdio.h>

int main()
{
    int max=5;
```

```
    for(int i=0;  i<max;  i++)
    {
        printf("i : %d\n", i);
    }

    return 0;
}
```

Listing 3.1 is straightforward: a main() function that initializes the integer-valued variable max (its value is 5), followed by a for loop that prints the integers between 0 and max.

The output from launching the C program in Listing 3.1 is here:

```
i : 0
i : 1
i : 2
i : 3
i : 4
```

WORKING WITH BREAK AND CONTINUE IN FOR LOOPS

Listing 3.2 displays the contents of BreakContinue.c that shows you how to use the break and continue statements in a for loop in C.

LISTING 3.2: BreakContinue.c

```
#include <stdio.h>

int main()
{
    int max=5;

    for(int i=0;  i<max;  i++)
    {
        if( i == 3 ) continue;
        if( i == 4 ) break;
        printf("i : %d\n", i);
    }

    return 0;
}
```

Listing 3.2 contains a for loop with conditional logic that checks the value of the loop variable i. If the value of i equals 3, the code "skips" to the top of the loop and increments the value of i. If the value of i equals 4, the code exits the loop and effectively ends the execution of the C program.

Thus, the only time that the printf() statement is executed is when the variable i equals 0, 1, or 2. The output from launching the C program in Listing 3.2 is here:

```
i : 0
i : 1
i : 2
```

CHECKING FOR LEAP YEARS

As a quick reminder, a *leap year* is a positive (integer-valued) year that satisfies the following two conditions:

- the year is a multiple of four, and
- if the year is a century then the year must be a multiple of 400

Examples of leap years include: 400, 1492, 1776, 2000, 2012, and 2472 (note that the centuries are multiples of 400). Examples of years that are not leap years include: 100, 1370, 1510, 1900, and 2011 (note that the centuries are *not* multiples of 400).

Listing 3.3 displays the contents of LeapYear.c that illustrates how to use if-else logic in a C program to determine if a particular year is a leap year.

LISTING 3.3: LeapYear.c

```c
#include <stdio.h>

int main()
{
    int years[6] = {1900, 1953, 1958, 2000, 2004, 2006};
    int year=0, leapyear=0;

    int len = sizeof(years)/sizeof(years[0]);

    for(int i=0; i<len; i++)
    {
        year = years[i];

        if( year % 4 == 0)
        {
            leapyear = 1;

            // "leap centuries" must be multiples of 400
            if( (year % 100 == 0) && (year % 400 != 0) )
            {
                leapyear = 0;
            }
        }
        else // not a multiple of 4
        {
            leapyear = 0;
        }

        if( leapyear == 0)
        {
            printf("%d: not a leap year\n",year);
        }
        else
        {
            printf("%d: leap year\n",year);
        }
    }
```

```
    return 0;
}
```

Listing 3.3 defines the "flag" variable `leapyear`, along with the integer-valued array `years` that contains six positive integers. Next, a `for` loop iterates through the elements of the years array in order to determine which year (if any) is a leap year.

The outer `if` statement checks if the current year is a multiple of 4: if so then it's a leap year (and `leapyear` is set to 1); if not, then the `else` clause sets `leapyear` to 0 (because it's not a leap year).

There is an additional check that must be performed. The inner `if` statement checks if the current year is a multiple of 100 *and not* a multiple of 400: if this is the case, then the current year is not a leap year, so the variable `leapyear` must be set to 0 (because its value has already been set to 1 by the outer `if` statement).

The bottom portion of the `for` loop contains conditional logic that displays the appropriate message based on the value of the variable `leapyear`.

The output from Listing 3.3 is here:

```
1900: not a leap year
1953: not a leap year
1958: not a leap year
2000: leap year
2004: leap year
2006: not a leap year
```

CHECKING ALPHABETIC TYPES

Letters and numbers have an ASCII value, and it's possible to check their type. Listing 3.4 displays the contents of `Alphabetic.c` that illustrates how to check for alphabetic characters in C.

LISTING 3.4: Alphabetic.c
```c
#include <stdio.h>
#include <ctype.h>

int main()
{
    int ch;

    for (ch = 0x7c; ch <= 0x82; ch++) {
        printf("%#04x      ", ch);

        if (isascii(ch))
        {
            printf("The character is %c\n", ch);
        }
        else
        {
            printf("Cannot be represented by an ASCII
                    character\n");
        }
```

```
      }

      return 0;
}
```

Listing 3.4 contains a `for` loop whose loop variable `ch` iterates from the value `0x7c` up to (and including) the value `0x82`. The conditional logic uses the value of the built-in function `isascii(ch)` to determine whether the value of `ch` is a printable character.

The output from compiling and executing the code in Listing 3.4 is here:

```
0x7c    The character is |
0x7d    The character is }
0x7e    The character is ~
0x7f    The character is
0x80    Cannot be represented by an ASCII character
0x81    Cannot be represented by an ASCII character
0x82    Cannot be represented by an ASCII character
```

COUNTING UPPERCASE AND LOWERCASE CHARACTERS

Listing 3.5 displays the contents of `UpperLowerCount.c` that illustrates how to count the number of uppercase and lowercase letters in a string.

LISTING 3.5: UpperLowerCount.c

```c
#include <stdio.h>
#include <string.h>

int main()
{
    char ch, str1[] = "This is a String";
    int lcount=0, ucount=0;

    int len1 = strlen(str1);

    for(int i=0; i<len1; i++)
    {
        ch = str1[i];
        if( ('a' <= ch) && (ch <= 'z'))
        {
            lcount++;
        }
        else if( ('A' <= ch) && (ch <= 'Z'))
        {
            ucount++;
        }
    }

    printf("Original:    %s\n",str1);
    printf("Lower count: %d\n",lcount);
    printf("Upper count: %d\n",ucount);

    return 0;
}
```

Listing 3.5 starts by defining the character string str1, and then initializing the integer-valued variable len1 with the length of the string str1. The next section in Listing 3.5 contains a for loop whose loop variable i iterates between 0 and len1, and initializes the variable ch with the character that is in the ith position of the str1 array.

Next, conditional logic checks if ch is between the letters "A" and "Z," in which case the variable lcount (which keeps track of the number of lowercase letters) is incremented.

If ch is between the letters "A" and "Z," in which case the variable ucount (which keeps track of the number of uppercase letters) is incremented.

The final portion of Listing 3.5 contains three printf() statements that display the original string str1, the number of lowercase letters, and the number of uppercase letters.

The output from compiling and executing the code in Listing 3.5 is here:

```
Original:    This is a String
Lower count: 11
Upper count: 2
```

CHECKING CHARACTER TYPES

Listing 3.6 displays the contents of TestChars.c that illustrates how to use some built-in functions in order to check for various character types in C.

LISTING 3.6: TestChars.c

```
#include <stdio.h>
#include <string.h>
#include <ctype.h>

int main()
{
   char ch, line[] = "Abc3 :";
   int i, count;

   count = strlen(line);

   for(i=0; i<count; i++)
   {
     ch = line[i];

     if(isblank(ch))
     {
        printf("%c is a blank\n", ch);
     }
     else if(isdigit(ch))
     {
        printf("%c is a digit\n", ch);
     }
     else if(isupper(ch))
     {
```

```
        printf("%c is uppercase\n", ch);
    }
    else if(islower(ch))
    {
        printf("%c is uppercase\n", ch);
    }
    else if(ispunct(ch))
    {
        printf("%c is punctuation\n", ch);
    }
    else
    {
        printf("%c is other type\n", ch);
    }
}

    return 0;
}
```

Listing 3.6 defines a string variable `line`, followed by a `for` loop that iterates through each character in the string `line`. Next, the if/else conditional logic invokes the built-in C functions `isblank(ch)`, `isdigit(ch)`, `isupper(ch)`, `islower(ch)`, and `ispunct(ch)` to check if a character is a blank, a digit, an uppercase letter, a lowercase letter, or punctuation, respectively. If the conditional check is true, then the appropriate text message is printed.

The output from compiling and executing the code in Listing 3.6 is here:

```
A is uppercase
b is uppercase
c is uppercase
3 is a digit
  is a blank
: is punctuation
```

Listing 3.6 contains an assortment of built-in functions for testing the type of a given character. In addition, C supports the following useful built-in character-related functions:

```
iscntrl()  Tests for control characters.
isgraph()  Tests for printable characters excluding the
space.
isprint()  Tests for printable characters including the
space.
ispunct()  Tests for punctuation characters as defined in
           the locale.
isspace()  Tests for white-space characters.
isxdigit() Tests for wide hexadecimal digits 0 through 9, a
           through f, or A through F.
```

WORKING WITH ARRAYS

As you saw in Chapter 1, an array declaration in C requires the type of the elements and the number of elements required by an array:

```
type arrayName [ arraySize ];
```

The preceding code snippet is for defining a one-dimensional array. The value of `arraySize` must be an integer constant greater than zero, and the `type` can be any valid C data type. For example, to declare a 10-element array called `balance` of type `double`, use this statement:

```
double balance[10];
```

As you can see, the `balance` array can hold as many as 10 `double` numbers, and the following subsections contain examples of working with the `balance` array.

Initializing Arrays

C arrays start with an index value of 0, and the index value of the last element in the array is the array size minus 1. C allows you to initialize the values in an array in two ways: either one element at a time or via a single statement. An example of the latter is here:

```
double balance[5] = {1.5, 2.0, 3.4, 997.0, 25.0};
```

Notice that the number of values inside the pair of braces { } equals the number that is specified inside the square brackets [ ]. You can also omit the size of the array, and the compiler will handle the initialization, an example of which is here:

```
double balance[] = {1.5, 2.0, 3.4, 997.0, 25.0, -123, 777};
```

After initializing an array, you can also update the value of an element, as shown here:

```
balance[2] = 3000.0;
```

Array Values

Access an array element via the index of the element in the array. For example, suppose the `balance` array is initialized as above:

```
double balance[5] = {1.5, 2.0, 3.4, 997.0, 25.0};
```

Then the third element has index two, and you can triple its value with this code snippet:

```
balance[2] *= 3;
```

Listing 3.7 displays the contents of `ArrayElems.c` that illustrates how to access elements in an array.

LISTING 3.7: ArrayElems.c
```
#include <stdio.h>
```

```
int main()
{
    int arr1[10];

    // initialize element i with value i+100
    for (int i=0; i<10; i++ )
    {
        arr1[i] = i + 100;
    }

    for (int j=0; j<10; j++ )
    {
        printf("Element[%d] = %d\n", j, arr1[j] );
    }

    return 0;
}
```

Listing 3.7 contains a main() function that defines the integer arr1 with 10 elements, followed by a loop that initializes each element to its index position plus 100. The second loop simply displays the values of each element in the array arr1. Launch the code in Listing 3.7 and you will see the following output:

```
Element[0] = 100
Element[1] = 101
Element[2] = 102
Element[3] = 103
Element[4] = 104
Element[5] = 105
Element[6] = 106
Element[7] = 107
Element[8] = 108
Element[9] = 109
```

C Functions and Arrays

C supports multi-dimensional arrays (discussed in the next section) that you can pass to functions (discussed in Chapter 4). You can also initialize a pointer to an array and pass that pointer to a function. Moreover, you can define C functions that return an array or a pointer to an array. As you will see later, you can initialize a pointer to the first element of an array simply by specifying the name of the array (without an index).

MULTI-DIMENSIONAL ARRAYS

Each of the following code snippets illustrates several ways to initialize a 2 x 3 array of integers in C:

```
int arr1[2]= {{1,2,3}, {4,5,6}};
int arr2[][3] = {{1,2,3}, {4,5,6}};
int arr3[2][3] = {1,2,3,4,5,6;
```

Listing 3.8 displays the contents of `MultiDimArray1.c` that shows you how to calculate the sum of the entries in a multi-dimensional array.

LISTING 3.8: MultiDimArray1.c

```c
#include <stdio.h>

int main()
{
    double total=0.0, rowSum=0.0;
    int row=2, col=3;
    int arr1[2]= {{1,2,3}, {4,5,6}};

    for(int i=0; i<row; i++)
    {
        rowSum=0.0;
        for(int j=0; j<col; j++)
        {
            total += arr1[i][j];
            rowSum += arr1[i][j];
        }

        printf("Sum of row %d: %f\n", i, rowSum);
    }

    printf("Total Sum: %f\n", total);

    return 0;
}
```

Listing 3.8 contains the variables `total` and `rowSum` that will store the sum of all the elements in an array and the sum of a row of elements, respectively. Next, the array `arr1` is a 2x3 array (that is, it consists of two rows and three columns) that is initialized with a set of values.

The next section in Listing 3.8 contains an outer `for` loop that iterates through the rows of `arr1`. After initializing `rowSum` to 0.0, an inner loop iterates through the columns of the current row. Notice that the `total` variable and the `rowSum` variables are both incremented by the quantity `arr1[i][j]`. When the inner loop has completed, the `printf()` statement displays the sum of the elements in the correct row.

Note that (unlike the variable `rowSum`) the variable `total` is not re-initialized to 0 because we want to compute the sum of all the elements in the array `arr1`. In fact, when the outer loop has finished execution, the bottom of the `main()` function in Listing 3.8 contains a `printf()` statement that prints the sum of all the elements. The output from Listing 3.8 is here:

```
Sum of row 0: 6.000000
Sum of row 1: 15.000000
Total Sum:    21.000000
```

Another point to keep in mind: C11 supports variable-length arrays but cannot be initialized. For example, if you use the variables row and col (with values 2 and 3, respectively) to define the dimensions of arr1, you will see the following error during compilation:

```
MultiDimArray1.c:7:13: error: variable-sized object may not
be initialized
    int arr1[row][col]={{1,2,3}, {4,5,6}};
            ^~~
1 error generated.
```

CALCULATING THE TRANSPOSE OF A SQUARE MATRIX

The transpose of a square matrix is the result of interchanging the row and column position. In other words, if the value of the element in the (i,j) position of matrix A is a(i,j), then the value of the element in the (i,j) position of the transpose of matrix A is a(j,i).

Listing 3.9 displays the contents of Transpose.c that illustrates how to calculate the transpose of a square matrix.

LISTING 3.9: Transpose.c

```
#include <stdio.h>

int main()
{
    int row=3, col=3, temp=0;
    int arr1[3]= {{1,2,3},
                  {4,5,6},
                  {7,8,9}};

    // display original matrix
    printf("Original\n");
    for(int i=0; i<row; i++)
    {
        printf("Row %d: ",i);
        for(int j=0; j<col; j++)
        {
            printf("%d ", arr1[i][j]);
        }
        printf("\n");
    }

    for(int i=1; i<row; i++)
    {
        for(int j=0; j<i; j++)
        {
            temp = arr1[i][j];
            arr1[i][j] = arr1[j][i];
            arr1[j][i] = temp;
        }
    }
```

```
// display transposed matrix
printf("Transpose\n");
for(int i=0; i<row; i++)
{
    printf("Row %d: ",i);
    for(int j=0; j<col; j++)
    {
        printf("%d ", arr1[i][j]);
    }
    printf("\n");
}

return 0;
}
```

Listing 3.9 contains a `main()` function that initializes several scalar variables, followed by initializing the 3x3 array `arr1` with integer values. Next, a nested loop displays the values in the array `arr1`.

The second loop contains a nested loop that "swaps" the entries in position `(i,j)` with position `(j,i)` by means of a temporary storage variable called `temp`. This code block is a standard technique that you will see in practically every programming language, so it's worthwhile committing the code to memory.

The third loop contains a nested loop that displays the new values in the array `arr1`. The output from Listing 3.9 is here:

```
Original
Row 0: 1 2 3
Row 1: 4 5 6
Row 2: 7 8 9
Transpose
Row 0: 1 4 7
Row 1: 2 5 8
Row 2: 3 6 9
```

As you can see, Listing 3.9 contains two identical blocks of code: a better solution is to use a function (discussed in Chapter 3) that prints the contents of an array.

LINEAR SEARCH IN ARRAYS

Listing 3.10 displays the contents of `LinearSearch.c` that shows you how to use a simple loop to determine whether or not a given integer is in a C array of integers.

LISTING 3.10: LinearSearch.c
```
#include <stdio.h>

int main()
{
```

```
int numbers[] = {15, 3, 99, -4, 25, 8};
int value = 25, pos = -1;

int count = sizeof(numbers)/sizeof(numbers[0]);

for(int i=0; i<count; i++)
{
   if(value == numbers[i])
   {
      pos = i;
      break;
   }
}

printf("Array: ");
for(int i=0; i<count; i++)
{
   printf("%d ", numbers[i]);
}
printf("\n");

printf("Value: %d\n",value);
printf("Pos:   %d\n",pos);

return 0;
}
```

Listing 3.10 contains a main() function that initializes a numbers array with 6 integers, as well as several scalar variables. Next, the code snippet (shown in bold) computes the size of the entire array divided by the size of the first element, which is assigned to the variable count. This value equals the number of elements in the array numbers.

The next section of code is a loop that iterates through the elements in the array numbers to search for an element equal to the variable value. If there is a match, then the index in the array is assigned to the variable pos. The final section of code displays value and pos (which is -1 if a match is not found). The output from Listing 3.10 is here:

```
Array: 15 3 99 -4 25 8
Value: 25
Pos:   4
```

REVERSING AN ARRAY OF NUMBERS

Listing 3.11 displays the contents of ReverseArray1.c that contains a for loop to reverse an array of numbers in a C program.

LISTING 3.11: ReverseArray1.c

```
#include <stdio.h>

int main()
```

```
{
    int numbers[6] = {15, 3, 99, -4, 25, 8};
    int reverse[6];
    int count=6;

    for(int i=0; i<count; i++)
    {
        reverse[count-1-i] = numbers[i];
    }

    printf("Array:    ");
    for(int i=0; i<count; i++)
    {
        printf("%d ", numbers[i]);
    }
    printf("\n");

    printf("Reverse: ");
    for(int i=0; i<count; i++)
    {
        printf("%d ", reverse[i]);
    }
    printf("\n");

    return 0;
}
```

Listing 3.11 contains a `main()` function that initializes a `numbers` array with 6 integers, then declares an array `reverse` for 6 integers, and then the `count` variable whose initial value is 6.

The first loop initializes the contents of the array reverse with the values in the numbers array in reverse order. For instance, `reverse[0]` is assigned `numbers[5]`, `reverse`is assigned `numbers[4]`, and so forth.

The second loop displays the contents of the `numbers` array, and the third loop displays the contents of the `reverse` array. The output from launching the C program in Listing 3.11 is here:

```
Array:    15 3 99 -4 25 8
Reverse: 8 25 -4 99 3 15
```

FINDING THE MAXIMUM AND MINIMUM IN ARRAYS

Listing 3.12 displays the contents of `MaxAndMinValue.c` that shows you how to use a simple loop (with conditional logic) in C in order to find the maximum and minimum values in an array.

LISTING 3.12: MaxAndMinValue.c

```
#include <stdio.h>

int main()
{
    int numbers[] = {15, 3, 99, -4, 25, 8};
```

```
int min=numbers[0], max=numbers[0];
int count=sizeof(numbers)/sizeof(numbers[0]);

for(int i=0; i<count; i++)
{
    if(min > numbers[i])
    {
        min = numbers[i];
    }

    if(max < numbers[i])
    {
        max = numbers[i];
    }
}

printf("Array: ");
for(int i=0; i<count; i++)
{
    printf("%d ", numbers[i]);
}
printf("\n");

printf("Max:    %d\n",max);
printf("Min:    %d\n",min);

return 0;
}
```

Listing 3.12 contains a `main()` function that initializes a `numbers` array with 6 integers, followed by the integer variables `min` and `max` that are both initialized with the value `numbers[0]`.

The first loop contains conditional logic that updates the value of `min` if the current element is smaller than `min`, and updates the value of `max` if the current element is larger than `max`. The second loop displays the values of the elements in the `numbers` array, and then displays the values of `min` and `max`. The output from launching the C program in Listing 3.12 is here:

```
Array: 15 3 99 -4 25 8
Max:    99
Min:    -4
```

DELETING AN ELEMENT FROM AN ARRAY

Listing 3.13 displays the contents of `DeleteArrayElement.c` that shows you how to use a `for` loop to delete an element from an array of numbers in a C program.

LISTING 3.13: DeleteArrayElement.c

```
#include <stdio.h>

int main()
```

```
{
    int pos = 4;
    int numbers[] = {15, 3, 99, -4, 25, 8};
    int count=sizeof(numbers)/sizeof(numbers[0]);

    printf("Initial: ");
    for(int i=0; i<count; i++)
    {
        printf("%d ",numbers[i]);
    }
    printf("\n");

    printf("Removed: %d\n",numbers[pos]);
    for(inti=pos; i<count-1; i++)
    {
        numbers[i] = numbers[i+1];
    }
    numbers[count-1] = 0;

    printf("Updated: ");
    for(int i=0; i<count; i++)
    {
        printf("%d ",numbers[i]);
    }
    printf("\n");

    return 0;
}
```

Listing 3.13 contains a main() function that initializes a numbers array with 6 integers, followed by the integer variable pos that specifies the index position of the numbers array that will be deleted.

The first loop displays the contents of the numbers array, followed by the second loop that performs the deletion. The loop essentially "shifts" the elements (that are to the right of position pos) one position to the left. For instance, since pos[4] will be deleted, we can replace its value by pos[5]. Next, replace pos[5] with the value of pos[6]. Repeat this process until we reach the last (right-most) element in the numbers array.

The final loop displays the updated contents of the numbers array. The output from launching the C program in Listing 3.13 is here:

```
Initial: 15 3 99 -4 25 8
Removed: 25
Updated: 15 3 99 25 8 0
```

STRINGS AND FOR LOOPS

Listing 3.14 displays the contents of ForLoopStr.c that shows you how to use a simple for loop to display the characters in a text string in a C program. This code sample contains a preview of the use of pointers in C, which are not discussed in detail until Chapter 5. If need be, feel free to skip this code sample until after you have read the material in Chapter 5.

LISTING 3.14: ForLoopStr.c

```c
#include <stdio.h>
#include <string.h>

int main()
{
    char *str = "hello";
    char *p = str;
    int len = strlen(str);

    printf("First Loop\n");
    printf("----------\n");
    for(int i=0; i<len; i++)
    {
        printf("i : %c\n", str[i]);
    }

    printf("\nSecond Loop\n");
    printf("----------\n");
    for(int i=0; i<len; i++)
    {
        printf("i : %s\n", p);
        ++p;
    }

    return 0;
}
```

Listing 3.14 contains a `main()` function that initializes the character pointer `str` to a hard-coded string, and then initializes the character pointer `p` to the address of `str`. The first loop displays each character in `str`, using the syntax `(char)str[i]`.

The second loop also displays substrings of `str`, this time using the syntax `(char *)p`. The pointer `p` starts at the address of `str`, and during each iteration of the `for` loop, the address of pointer `p` is incremented by the code snippet `++p` (which can also be combined with the previous code snippet). As the pointer `p` "advanced" through each position of `str`, the output is a shorter substring. The output from Listing 3.14 is here:

```
First Loop
----------
i : h
i : e
i : l
i : l
i : o

Second Loop
-----------
i : hello
i : ello
i : llo
i : lo
i : o
```

COUNTING WORDS IN A LINE OF TEXT

Listing 3.15 displays the contents of CountWords.c that illustrates how to count the number of words in a line of text (words are separated by a blank or a tab character).

LISTING 3.15: CountWords.c

```c
#include <stdio.h>
#include <stdlib.h>
#include <string.h>
#include <ctype.h>

int main()
{
   char str1[] = "  This is a    String";
   int i=0, wCount=0;

   int len1 = strlen(str1);

   // skip over leading whitespace
   for(i=0; i<len1; i++)
   {
     if((str1[i]!=' ')&&(str1[i]!='\t'))
     {
        break;
     }
   }

   for(; i<len1; i++)
   {
      // found a whitespace => found a word
      if((str1[i]==' ')||(str1[i]=='\t'))
      {
         wCount++;
      }

      // handle the case where there are
      // multiple whitespaces between words
   }

   wCount++;

   printf("Line of Text:  %s\n",str1);
   printf("Word Count:    %d\n",wCount);

   return 0;
}
```

Listing 3.15 contains a main() function that initializes the character string str1 to a hard-coded string, and then initializes some scalar values. The first loop skips any initial whitespaces (which can be a simple space or a tab character).

The second loop increments the variable wCount each time that a whitespace is encountered in str1. The underlying assumption is that the occurrence of a whitespace implies the existence of a new word. However, if there are multiple whitespaces between words, *you need to modify this code to skip those "extra" whitespaces*, in much the same way that the initial whitespaces are skipped (it's an exercise for you). The output from launching CountWords is here:

```
Line of Text:   This is a    String
Word Count:     6
```

WORKING WITH NESTED FOR LOOPS

Listing 3.16 displays the contents of NestedForLoop.c that shows you how to use a nested for loop in a C program.

LISTING 3.16: NestedForLoop.c

```c
#include <stdio.h>

int main()
{
    int max=5;

    for(int i=0; i<max; i++)
    {
        printf("(i,j) : ");
        for(int j=0; j<max; j++)
        {
            printf("%d %d ", i, j);
        }
        printf("\n");
    }

    return 0;
}
```

Listing 3.16 contains a main() function with a nested loop that iterates through the numbers between 0 and 4 inclusive, and uses the printf() function to display the current (i,j) position (where i is the index of the outer loop and j is the index of the inner loop). The output from Listing 3.16 is here:

```
(i,j) : 0,0 0,1 0,2 0,3 0,4
(i,j) : 1,0 1,1 1,2 1,3 1,4
(i,j) : 2,0 2,1 2,2 2,3 2,4
(i,j) : 3,0 3,1 3,2 3,3 3,4
(i,j) : 4,0 4,1 4,2 4,3 4,4
```

The next section shows you how to work with while loops in C programs.

WORKING WITH WHILE LOOPS

Listing 3.17 displays the contents of WhileLoop.c that shows you how to use a while loop in order to print a single column of integers in C.

LISTING 3.17: WhileLoop.c

```
#include <stdio.h>

int main()
{
    int i=0, max=5;
    while(i<max)
    {
        printf("i : %d\n", i);
        ++i;
    }

    return 0;
}
```

Listing 3.17 contains a main() function that initializes the variables i and max with the values 0 and 5, respectively. The next section of code is a while loop that executes as long as the value of i is less than 5. Inside the body of the loop the printf() function displays the current value of i, after which the value of i is incremented. The output from launching Listing 3.17 is here:

```
i : 0
i : 1
i : 2
i : 3
i : 4
```

READING AN ENTIRE LINE FROM THE COMMAND LINE

Listing 3.18 displays the contents of ReadEntireLine.c that illustrates how to read an entire input line from standard input in a C program.

LISTING 3.18: ReadEntireLine.c

```
#include <stdio.h>

#define LINE_SIZE 100

int main()
{
    int charCount=0, inputChar;
    char line[LINE_SIZE];
    char lineFeed = '\n';

    while( (inputChar = getchar()) != lineFeed )
    {
```

```
    if(charCount < LINE_SIZE)
    {
        line[charCount] = inputChar;
    }

    charCount++;
  }

  printf("Input length = %d\n", charCount);

  return 0;
}
```

Listing 3.18 is similar to a code sample in Chapter 2. The difference is that this code contains a `while` loop that "populates" a character array with users until a linefeed is detected, at which point the `while` loop will stop execution. In addition, a maximum of 100 characters (the value of `LINE_SIZE`) will be accepted as input, after which the `while` loop stops putting elements in the array. The next portion of Listing 3.18 displays the number of characters that users typed. An example of the output from Listing 3.18 is here:

```
this is a line
Input length = 14
```

THE SWITCH STATEMENT

This section shows you how to use the C `switch` statement in order to print a text string that corresponds to a randomly generated number (that is generated via the `rand()` function). Note that you need to seed the random number generator using `srand()` in order to use a value different from 1 (the default value). Each time that you run this code, a different value is generated.

Note that if you add a loop to this program and invoke the `rand()` function inside the loop, a different result is generated, even without seeding the random number generator.

Listing 3.19 displays the contents of `Switch.c` that shows you how to use a `switch` statement in C programs.

LISTING 3.19: Switch.c

```
#include <stdio.h>
#include <stdlib.h>
#include <time.h>

int main()
{
    // seed the random number generator:
    srand(time(NULL));

    int rnd = rand() % 6 + 1;

    switch(rnd)
```

```
    {
        case 1:    printf("ONE\n");
                   break;
        case 2:    printf("TWO\n");
                   break;
        case 3:    printf("THREE\n");
                   break;
        case 4:    printf("FOUR\n");
                   break;
        case 5:    printf("FIVE\n");
                   break;
        case 6:    printf("SIX\n");
                   break;
        default:   printf("Other value\n");
    }

    return 0;
}
```

Listing 3.19 contains a main() function that invokes the built-in srand() C function to "seed" an initial random number, which will be different each time you launch the code in this section.

Next, the integer variable rnd is initialized with a random integer between 1 and 6 inclusive. The next portion of code consists of a switch() statement that displays a message based on the value of the variable rnd. The output from launching the code in Listing 3.19 several times is here:

```
Switch
FOUR
Switch
ONE
Switch
TWO
```

If you "comment out" the code snippet for srand() in Listing 3.23, the new output will be something like this:

```
Switch
TWO
Switch
TWO
Switch
TWO
```

Alternatively you could place the switch() statement inside a while loop, with the appropriate exit condition, in order to generate multiple output values (instead of launching the code multiple times).

WORKING WITH ARRAYS OF NUMBERS

Listing 3.20 displays the contents of Factorial2.c that illustrates how to calculate the factorial value of a positive integer using an iterative solution.

LISTING 3.20: Factorial2.c

```
#include <stdio.h>

int main()
{
    int result=1, num=5;

    for(int i=1; i<=num; i++)
    {
        result *= i;
    }

    printf("%d factorial = %d\n", num, result);

    return 0;
}
```

Listing 3.20 defines the variable result (which will contain the calculated factorial value) and num (which is the number whose factorial value we want to calculate). The next portion of Listing 3.24 is a for loop whose loop variable i ranges between 1 and num, and each iteration through that loop multiplies the value of result with the value of i, thereby computing the factorial value of num.

The output from Listing 3.20 is here:

```
5 factorial = 120
```

Chapter 4 contains a recursive solution for calculating the factorial value of a positive integer.

WORKING WITH ARRAYS OF STRINGS

Listing 3.21 displays the contents of ArrayOfStrings.c that shows you how to define and populate an array of strings in a C program.

LISTING 3.21: ArrayOfStrings.c

```
#include <stdio.h>
#include <string.h>

int main()
{
    char names[3][20];

    strcpy(names[0], "Jane Smith");
    strcpy(names[1], "John Edwards");
    strcpy(names[2], "Steve Anderson");

    for(int i=0; i<3; i++)
    {
        printf("Name: %s\n", names[i]);
    }
```

```
      return 0;
}
```

Listing 3.21 contains a `main()` function that initializes the 3x20 character array names, followed by three `strcpy()` invocations that populate the three rows of the names array.

The next section of code is a loop that displays the contents of each row of the names array. The output from launching Listing 3.21 is here:

```
Name:  Jane Smith
Name:  John Edwards
Name:  Steve Anderson
```

USING A WHILE LOOP TO FIND THE DIVISORS OF A NUMBER

Listing 3.22 contains a `while` loop, conditional logic, and the `%` (modulus) operator in order to find the factors of any integer greater than 1.

LISTING 3.22: Divisors.c

```c
#include <stdio.h>

int main()
{
   int div=2, num=12;

   printf("Number: %d\n", num);

   while(num > 1)
   {
      if(num % div == 0)
      {
         printf("divisor: %d\n", div);
         num /= div;
      }
      else
      {
         ++div;
      }
   }

   return 0;
}
```

Listing 3.22 defines an integer `num` with the value 12 and initializes the variable `div` with the value 2. The `while` loop divides `num` by `div` and if the remainder is 0, it prints the value of `div` and then it divides `num` by `div`; if the value is not 0, then `div` is incremented by 1. This `while` loop continues as long as `num` is greater than 1.

The output from Listing 3.22 that finds the divisors of 12 is here:

```
Number: 12
divisor: 2
divisor: 2
divisor: 3
```

Why does the code Listing 3.22 find only prime divisors and not composite divisors? The code works correctly because of the `if` statement. For example, 6 will never be printed as a divisor of 12 because the code initially determines that 2 is a prime divisor of 12, and then the `if` code block reduces the original number from 12 to 6. Next, the code determines that 2 is a prime divisor of 6, and then the `if` code block replaces 6 with 3. Finally, 3 is a prime divisor of 3, after which 3 is replaced with 1, whereupon the `while` loop is terminated.

USING A WHILE LOOP TO FIND PRIME NUMBERS

Listing 3.23 contains a `while` loop, conditional logic, and the % (modulus) operator in order to count the number of prime factors of any integer greater than 1. If there is only one divisor for a number, then that number is a prime number.

LISTING 3.23: Divisors3.c

```c
#include <stdio.h>

int main()
{
    int count=1, div=2, num=12;

    while(div < num)
    {
        if(num % div == 0)
        {
            ++count;
        }

        ++div;
    }

    if(count == 1)
    {
        printf("%d is prime\n", num);
    }
    else
    {
        printf("%d is composite\n", num);
    }

    return 0;
}
```

Listing 3.23 initializes the variables `count`, `div`, `num` with the values 1, 2, and 12, respectively. The next section of code is a `while` loop that iterates as long as the value of `div` is less than the value of `num`.

Inside the while loop the value of `count` is incremented if `div` is a divisor of `num` (i.e., `num % div == 0`), after which `div` is unconditionally incremented.

After the `while` loop exits, a `printf()` statement displays a message that `num` is either prime or composite, depending on whether or not the value of `count` is 1. The output from launching Listing 3.17 is here:

```
12 is composite
```

SUMMARY

This chapter introduced you to `for` loops, single-dimension and multi-dimensional arrays, and how to perform a linear search in arrays. Next you learned how to find the maximum and minimum in an array of numbers, how to insert an element, and how to delete an element from an array.

You also saw how to work with `while` loops, `do-while` loops, and string-related examples involving `while` loops. In addition, you learned about conditional logic in C programs, such as if statements and if-else statements. You then learned how to find the divisors of a number, as well as how to check if a number is prime.

FUNCTIONS IN C

T his chapter introduces you to some built-in C functions and shows you how to create custom functions in C programs. You will also learn about recursion and how to define custom functions in order to solve various well-known tasks using recursion in C.

The first part of this chapter briefly discusses various types of built-in functions that are available in C. You have already seen some built-in functions (such as `isalpha()` and `ispunct()`) in earlier chapters, and this section contains other useful built-in functions. The second part of this chapter contains code samples that illustrate how to create C programs containing custom functions that use some of the built-in functions in C.

The third part of this chapter shows you how to use recursion in order to calculate factorial values, Fibonacci numbers, and the GCD (greatest common divisor) of a pair of integers using Euclid's algorithm (which relies on recursion). Although recursion is often considered an advanced topic in programming languages, recursion can be used for solving many problems in a simple and elegant fashion.

The final portion of this chapter shows you techniques for sorting an array of numbers and searching for a number in an array of numbers.

WORKING WITH BUILT-IN FUNCTIONS IN C

The built-in functions in C can return any of the supported C types, such as character, strings, pointers, pointers to functions, and so forth. All the C programs in this book contain a `main()` function that always returns an `int` type. What is the significance of this return value? You need information (i.e., some form of documentation, even if it's just a comment block) that describes the purpose of different values for a given return type.

However, some C functions do not return any value, in which case they have a return type of `void`. Note that some languages (such as Fortran) make a distinction between functions that return a value (they're called functions) and functions that do not return anything (they're called subroutines), but C does not make such a distinction.

Yet another scenario involves "call by reference" versus "call by value," which you will sometimes see in functions that have return type of `void`. The idea is straightforward: the former involves passing a memory location (i.e., a reference) of an argument to a function, whereas the latter involves passing a complete copy of an argument to a function. Both options are in the next section.

Pass by Reference versus Pass by Value

A C function that invokes another function by passing an "updateable" parameter is known as "pass-by-reference." This means that any changes to such an argument in the "called" function are reflected in the "calling" function. If a function contains a parameter that is a pointer to a memory location, then updates in the "called function" to that parameter are available in the "called function." For example, passing the address of a large memory block is more efficient than either 1) passing the contents of that memory block to a function, or 2) requiring the "called function" return a large modified memory block.

On the other hand, passing arguments that cannot be modified in a "called function" is known as "pass-by-value." Regardless of the calculations that are performed in the "called function," the parameters that are passed to that function retain their original values in the "calling function."

In general, use pass-by-value for primitive data types or fairly small memory blocks. If you decide to use pass-by-value for an argument, that involves a pointer (discussed in Chapter 5 and Chapter 6); hence, use extra care when doing so in order to avoid bugs. As already mentioned in the previous section, if a "called function" makes various updates to a large block of memory, then pass-by-reference makes sense because it's more efficient than pass-by-value.

Except for some code samples in Chapter 7, the code samples in the other chapters involve pass-by-value functions. In the meantime, the following subsections contain lists of built-in functions according to their type.

Built-in Character Functions

C supports a variety of convenient built-in functions to perform various tests on a character, such as determining whether a character is alphanumeric, alphabetic, a control character, a numeric digit, or a lowercase or uppercase letter. Here is a list of many of those functions (all of which have a return type of `int`), along with a brief description (many functions are intuitively named functions):

- int isalnum(int c): tests if c is alphanumeric
- int isalpha(int c): tests if c is alphabetic
- int iscntrl(int c): tests if c is a control character

- int isdigit(int c): tests if c is a numeric digit
- int islower(int c): tests if c is a lowercase character
- int isupper(int c): tests if c is an uppercase character
- int isgraph(int c): returns nonzero if c is any character for which either isalnum or ispunct returns nonzero.
- int isprint(int c): returns nonzero if c is space or a character for which isgraph returns nonzero.
- int ispunct(int c): returns nonzero if c is punctuation
- int isspace(int c): returns nonzero if c is space character
- int isxdigit(int c): returns nonzero if c is hexa digit
- int tolower(int c): returns the corresponding lowercase letter if one exists and if isupper(c): otherwise, it returns c.
- int toupper(int c): returns the corresponding uppercase letter if one exists and if islower(c): otherwise, it returns c.

Since the preceding functions are fairly straightforward, and you can easily find code samples online, we'll skip a code sample for this section and go directly to the next section, which provides a list of string-oriented built-in functions in C.

Converting Between Data Types

In some cases, it's possible to convert from one data type to another data type in C. The standard header file `stdlib.h` (header files are discussed in Chapter 7) provides all the string conversion functions in C.

For example, the functions `atof()`, `atoi()`, and `atol()` convert an ASCII value to a float, integer, and long value, respectively.

This concludes the section of the chapter pertaining to string-oriented built-in C functions. The next section provides a simple introduction to user-defined C functions.

DEFINING A SIMPLE CUSTOM FUNCTION

C functions have the following format: every function definition has a return type (which can be void), a name, zero or more arguments, and a function body. The preceding statement can be expressed via the following code snippet:

```
return-type function-name(argument declarations)
{
    declarations and statements
}
```

If a function does not return anything, then its `return-type` is void. Functions that *do* return something have the following type of statement in the function (not necessarily at the end of the function):

```
return (return-value)
```

Function Prototypes

A function prototype specifies the arguments (and their types) and the return type of a function. Although older versions of C did not require function prototypes, it's a good idea to include them because they allow the compiler to check that the data types of the passed parameters are compatible with the data types of the declared arguments.

An example of a function prototype is here:

```
void findChar(char str[], char c);
```

Function prototypes can be placed in a so-called header file that (by convention) has a .h suffix. The "header" file is then included (via a #include directive) in the C program that requires the function prototype. This technique improves code modularization and code re-use, which in turn enables to you create libraries for your projects.

As a simple example of creating a header file and including that header file in a C program, suppose that the file FindMain2.h contains the following code:

```
#include <ctype.h>
#include <stdio.h>

void findChar(char str[], char c);
```

You can reference FindMain2.h in the file FindMain2.c as follows:

```
#include "FindChar2.h"
```

This type of "separation" of files with function prototypes and implementation code is analogous to an interface file and an implementation file in Java. Although you probably won't use it until you have progressed beyond the beginner stage, it's good to be aware of this functionality.

FUNCTION PARAMETERS IN C FUNCTIONS

Function parameters are formal parameters, and they are treated as local variables within the function where they appear. In addition, such parameters take precedence over the global variables.

Listing 4.1 displays the contents of FunctionParams.c that illustrates the use of local and global variables in a C program.

LISTING 4.1: FunctionParams.c

```
#include <stdio.h>

// global variable declaration
int a = 20;

// function to add two integers
int sum(int a, int b)
```

```
{
    printf ("value of a in sum() = %d\n",  a);
    printf ("value of b in sum() = %d\n",  b);

    return a + b;
}

int main()
{
    // local variable declaration in main function
    int a = 10;
    int b = 20;
    int c = 0;

    printf ("value of a in main() = %d\n",  a);
    c = sum( a, b);
    printf ("value of c in main() = %d\n",  c);

    return 0;
}
```

Listing 4.1 starts by initializing the global variable a with the value 20, followed by the definition of the function sum() that takes two parameters. This function displays the values of the parameters and then returns their sum.

Next, the main() function initializes three local variables a, b, and c with the values 10, 20, and 0, respectively. The value of a is displayed, followed by an invocation of sum() whose return value is assigned to the variable c. The best way to trace the execution logic is to launch the code and note the displayed values (did you predict the same results?)

Launch the code in Listing 4.1 and you will see the following output:

```
value of a in main() = 10
value of a in sum() = 10
value of b in sum() = 20
value of c in main() = 30
```

Notice that the global value of a does not appear in the preceding output (do you know why?)

C99 SYNTAX FOR USER-DEFINED FUNCTIONS IN C

Chapter 1 briefly mentioned the C99 version of the C programming language. This section contains a code sample that illustrates one of the requirements of C99 for user-defined functions. If you refer to a function before the function is defined, you need to specify a "function prototype" before the location of the function call. By convention, these declarations appear near the beginning of the C program, typically before all function definitions.

Listing 4.2 displays the contents of SimpleC99.c that illustrates how to specify a function prototype (shown in bold) for the custom function message().

LISTING 4.2: Simplec99.c

```
#include <stdio.h>

// prevent "Implicit declaration of function is invalid
// in C99"
void message();

int main()
{
   message();

   return 0;
}

void message()
{
   printf("Hello from message\n");
}
```

Listing 4.2 contains a prototype for the function message() that has return type void and is defined later in the code. Next, the main() function invokes the message() function, which simply displays the text string Hello from message.

Compile and launch the code in Listing 4.2 and you will see the expected output:

```
Hello from message
```

One other point to keep in mind: if you place the definition of the message() function (and any other custom functions) *before* the definition of the main() function, then you do not need to include function prototypes.

K&R STYLE FUNCTION DEFINITIONS

Listing 4.3 displays the contents of OldStyleFunction.c that illustrates how to define a function using the K&R style for functions.

LISTING 4.3: OldStyleFunction.c

```
#include <stdio.h>

float perimeter(width, height)
int width;
float height;
{
   return 2 * (width + height);
}

int main()
{
   float perim = perimeter(10.0, 5);
```

```
    printf("Perimeter = %f\n", perim);

    return (0);
}
```

Listing 4.3 starts with the definition of the `perimeter()` function that returns the perimeter of a rectangle of dimensions width x height. Notice how the `width` and `height` parameters are declared (shown in bold).

Next, the `main()` function invokes the `perimeter()` function and assigns the returns value to the float variable `perim`.

The output from launching 4.3 is here:

```
Perimeter = 50.000000
```

K&R-style C allows for function prototypes; however, only the return type can be declared and the parameter list must be `()`, as shown here:

```
extern float atof();
```

The `()` in the preceding code snippet indicates that this function takes an unknown number of parameters of an unknown type.

CONVERTING STRINGS TO INTEGERS AND FLOAT VALUES

Listing 4.4 displays the contents of `ConvertDataTypes.c` that illustrates how to use the `sprintf()` to format and print various data values.

LISTING 4.4: *ConvertDataTypes.c*

```c
#include <stdlib.h>
#include <stdio.h>

int main()
{
    int i;
    long l;
    double x;
    char *s;

    s = " -2309.12E-15";
    x = atof(s); /* x = -2309.12E-15 */

    printf("x = %.4e\n",x);


    s = " -9885";
    i = atoi(s);       /* i = -9885 */

    printf("i = %d\n",i);
```

```
    s = "98854 dollars";
    l = atol(s);        /* l = 98854 */

    printf("l = %.ld\n",l);

    return (0);
}
```

Listing 4.4 starts by defining the variables i, 1, x, and s that are of type int, long, double, and char pointer, respectively. Then the variable s is initialized, and the built-in atoi() C function is invoked with the argument s and the result is assigned to the variable x, and then the value of x is displayed. This sequence of steps is performed with another value of s, and this time the output from the atoi() function is assigned to the value of i (whose value is displayed). The third sequence of steps is performed with a third value of s, and the result of invoking the atoi() function is assigned to the value l (whose value is displayed). The output from executing the code in Listing 4.5 is here:

```
x = -2.3091e-12
i = -9885
l = 98854
```

The following link contains code that enables you to convert an integer to a different base:

http://www.strudel.org.uk/itoa/#newest

PRINTING A STRING TO A BUFFER WITH SPRINTF()

The sprintf() function enables you to write numbers and characters to a buffer, with support for formats that are the same as those for the printf() function. In addition, every invocation of the sprintf() function returns the number of bytes that were written in the array (excluding the final null character), which enables you to keep track of the number of characters that were written to a buffer.

Listing 4.5 displays the contents of PrintToBuffer.c that illustrates how to use the sprintf() to format and print various data.

LISTING 4.5: PrintToBuffer.c

```
#include <stdio.h>

char buffer[200];
int i, j;
double fp;
char *s = "baltimore";
char c;

int main()
{
    c = 'l';
    i = 35;
```

```
fp = 1.7320508;

// Format and print various data
j  = sprintf(buffer,    "%s\n", s);
j += sprintf(buffer+j, "%c\n", c);
j += sprintf(buffer+j, "%d\n", i);
j += sprintf(buffer+j, "%f\n", fp);

printf("string:\n%s\ncharacter count = %d\n", buffer,
j);

return (0);
}
```

Listing 4.5 defines several variables of different type, after which the built-in `sprintf()` C function is invoked to copy the contents of the string s into buffer. This process is repeated with the variables c, i, and fp. The final code snippet displays the contents of buffer and the value of j. The output from executing the code in Listing 4.5 is here:

```
string:
baltimore
1
35
1.732051

character count = 24
```

Buffer Manipulation Functions

Earlier in the chapter you learned about built-in C functions, and this section contains additional C functions. The format is a terse one-sentence description, followed by the built-in C function (along with parameters and return value).

For example, you can copy n characters from ct to s and return s (s may be corrupted if objects overlap) with the following function:

```
void* memcpy(void* s, const void* ct, int n);
```

Compare the first n characters of cs and ct and return a negative value if cs < ct; return the value if they are equal; return a positive value if cs > ct:

```
int memcmp(const void* cs, const void* ct, int n);
```

Return a pointer to first occurrence of c in first n characters of cs, or NULL if not found:

```
void* memchr(const void* cs, int c, int n);
```

Replace each of the first n characters of s by c and return s:

```
void* memset(void* s, int c, int n);
```

Copy n characters from ct to s and return s (s will *not* be corrupted if objects overlap):

```c
void* memmove(void* s, const void* ct, int n);
```

You won't necessarily need to use all these built-in C functions, and you might frequently use a subset of them (it depends on the type of C programs that you need to write).

PASSING A ONE-DIMENSIONAL ARRAY AS AN ARGUMENT

Listing 4.7 displays the contents of SingleArrayFunction.c that illustrates how to pass a one-dimensional array to a function in a C program. Notice that the custom function addAll() is placed before the definition of the main() function, which means that a function prototype is not required for C99 compliance.

LISTING 4.7: SingleArrayFunction.c

```c
#include <stdio.h>

int addAll(int arr[], int size)
{
    int sum=0;

    for(int i=0; i<size; i++)
    {
        sum += arr[i];
    }

    return sum;
}

int main()
{
    // int array with 8 elements
    int arr1[8] = {1,2,3,4,5,6,7,8};
    int sum=0;

    printf("Values: ");
    for(int i=0; i<8; i++)
    {
        printf("%d ",arr1[i]);
    }
    printf("\n");

    sum = addAll(arr1,8);

    // output the returned value */
    printf("Sum = %d\n", sum);

    return 0;
}
```

Listing 4.7 defines the function addAll() that takes an integer array and an integer as parameters and returns an integer, which is the sum of the elements in the array. Next, the main() function contains a loop that displays the elements of the array arr1, followed by an invocation of the addAll() function whose return value is assigned to the variable sum. The last section of the main() method simply prints the value of sum. The output from Listing 4.7 is here:

```
Values: 1 2 3 4 5 6 7 8
Sum = 36
```

FINDING A CHARACTER IN A STRING

Listing 4.8 displays the contents of FindChar1.c that shows you how to find the number of occurrences of a character in a given string in a C program.

LISTING 4.8: FindChar1.c

```c
#include <ctype.h>
#include <stdio.h>

void findChar(char str[], char c)
{
    int matchCount = 0;

    printf("String: %s\n",str);
    printf("Char:   %c\n",c);

    for(int i=0; str[i]; i++)
    {
        if(str[i] == c)
        {
            printf("Match in position: %d\n",i);
            ++matchCount;
        }
    }

    printf("Count:   %d\n\n",matchCount);
}

int main()
{
    char str1[] = "pasta";
    findChar(str1, 'a');

    char str2[] = "New York City";
    findChar(str2, 'k');

    char str3[] = "California";
    findChar(str3, 'z');

    return (0);
}
```

Listing 4.8 defines the function findChar() that takes a character string and a character as parameters and has a return type of void. This function iterates through the character string and counts the number of occurrences of the character c. Each time a match is found a message is displayed, followed by a message with the number of occurrences of c in the string.

The main() function defines three character strings str1, str2, and str3, and invokes the findChar() method with each of these strings, along with the character a, k, and z, respectively. The output from Listing 4.9 is here:

```
String: pasta
Char:    a
Match in position: 1
Match in position: 4
Count:   2

String: New York City
Char:    k
Match in position: 7
Count:   1

String: California
Char:    z
Count:   0
```

CONVERTING STRINGS TO DECIMAL VALUES

This section contains an example of built-in functions in C that enable you to test the characters in a string to determine whether they are digits.

LISTING 4.9: DisplayDigits.c

```c
#include <ctype.h>
#include <stdio.h>

void checkDigits(char str[])
{
   printf("Number: %s\n",str);

   for(int i=0; str[i]; i++)
   {
      if(isdigit(str[i]))
      {
         printf("Digit: %c\n",str[i]);
      }
      else
      {
         printf("Not Digit: %c\n",str[i]);
      }
   }

   printf("\n");
}
```

```
int main()
{
    char str1[] = "123.456";
    checkDigits(str1);
    char str2[] = "-51.203";
    checkDigits(str2);

    return (0);
}
```

Listing 4.9 defines the function checkDigits() that takes a character string and has a return type of void. This function iterates through the character string and uses conditional logic, with the built-in C function isdigit(), to determine whether each character is a digit, and print a suitable message.

The main() function defines two character strings str1 and str2 and invokes the checkDigits() function with each of these strings. The output from Listing 4.9 is here:

```
Number: 123.456
Digit: 1
Digit: 2
Digit: 3
Not Digit: .
Digit: 4
Digit: 5
Digit: 6

Number: -51.203
Not Digit: -
Digit: 5
Digit: 1
Not Digit: .
Digit: 2
Digit: 0
Digit: 3
```

DISPLAY A LIST OF PRIME NUMBERS

Listing 4.10 displays the contents of DisplayPrimes.c that shows you how to define invoke a custom function isPrime() that is invoked from a for loop that is inside the main() function in order to display a list of prime numbers. Although you can place the code for the function isPrime() inside a loop in the main() function, the use of a function enables you to modularize the code.

LISTING 4.10: DisplayPrimes.c

```
#include <stdio.h>

int isPrime(int idx)
{
    int flag=0, div=2;
```

```c
    while (div <= idx/2)
    {
        if (idx % div == 0) // composite
        {
            flag = 1;
            break;
        }
        div++;
    }

    return flag;
}


int main()
{
    int maxVal=50, idx=0, result=0;

    for (idx=1; idx<=maxVal; idx++)
    {
        result = isPrime(idx);

        if ( result == 0) // prime
        {
            printf("%d ", idx);
        }
    }

    return 0;
}
```

Listing 4.10 contains the function isPrime() that returns 0 if a number is prime and returns 1 if a number is composite. The isPrime() function contains a for loop that starts at 2 and ends at idx /2, and checks whether or not any of these numbers are divisors of the number idx. If so, then the flag variable (which is initialized with the value 0) is set to 1 and the code exits the loop; otherwise the loop terminates normally. In either case, the isPrime() function returns the value of flag.

Next, the body of the main() function contains a for loop whose loop variable idx iterates from 1 to maxVal (which is initialized as 50). Each iteration through the for loop invokes the isPrime() function with the current value of idx. The next portion of the for loop prints the value of idx only if idx is prime (i.e., isPrime() returns a 0).

The output from Listing 4.10 is here:

```
1 2 3 5 7 11 13 17 19 23 29 31 37 41 43 47
```

This concludes the discussion of custom functions in C programs. The next portion of this chapter introduces you to recursion, along with some code samples that illustrate how to use recursion in C.

WHAT IS RECURSION?

Recursion is a powerful technique that can provide an elegant solution to various problems, such as factorial values, Fibonacci numbers, and the GCD of two positive integers via the Euclidean algorithm.

One interesting (and perhaps counterintuitive) fact: the expressive power of recursion-based algorithms is the same as that of iterative algorithms (i.e., neither type of algorithm is more "powerful" than the other one). However, there is a sort of asymmetry involved when working with algorithms to solve various tasks. For instance, the task of calculating Fibonacci numbers via recursion is straightforward, whereas an interactive solution is far from obvious. An even more interesting task is called the Tower of Hanoi, which can be solved in a very elegant manner via a recursive algorithm. If you feel sufficiently motivated, try implementing the solution via an iterative algorithm (and good luck with that!).

Yet another task that can be solved in an elegant manner involves the recursive definition of Ackermann functions, which has a "two-dimensional" recursion that makes it more complex (more interesting?) than the typical "one-dimensional" recursion that you will find in common recursion-based tasks. Ackermann functions are outside the scope of this book, but details about Ackermann functions are available through an Internet search.

However, let's not dismiss the suitability of iterative solutions for recursion-based tasks. For example, the definition of the factorial value of a non-negative integer is recursive, yet its iterative solution is very straightforward and elegant in its simplicity (if we ignore storage requirements). The takeaway point is simple: use the algorithm that works best for your requirements, keeping in mind the performance cost, code maintenance, and feature enhancements.

With the preceding points in mind, let's look at some examples of using recursion to calculate some well-known numbers, which are discussed in detail in the following subsections.

Calculating Factorial Values

The factorial value of a positive integer n is the product of all the integers between 1 and n. The symbol for factorial is the exclamation point ("!") and some sample factorial values are here:

```
1! = 1
2! = 2
3! = 6
4! = 20
5! = 120
```

The formula for the factorial value of a number is succinctly defined as follows:

```
Factorial(n) = n*Factorial(n-1) for n > 1 and
Factorial(1) = 1
```

Chapter 3 showed you how to use a `for` loop to calculate the factorial value of a positive integer. Listing 4.11 displays the contents of `Factorial.c` that illustrates how to use recursion in order to calculate the factorial value of a positive integer.

LISTING 4.11: Factorial.c

```c
#include <stdio.h>

int factorial(int num)
{
    if(num > 1)
    {
        return num*factorial(num-1);
    }
    else
    {
        return 1;
    }
}

int main()
{
    int result=0, num=5;
    result = factorial(num);

    printf("%d factorial = %d\n", num, result);

    return (0);
}
```

Listing 4.11 contains the function `factorial` that implements the recursive definition of the factorial value of a number, as described at the beginning of this section. The function `factorial()` recursively "drills down" by successively invoking itself until its parameter value is 1, in which case the number 1 is returned. Each "drill down" also multiplies the recursive function invocation by successively smaller integers, thereby "accumulating" the product of the numbers between 1 and num.

The output from Listing 4.11 is here:

```
5 factorial = 120
```

CALCULATING FIBONACCI NUMBERS VIA RECURSION

The set of Fibonacci numbers represent some interesting patterns (such as the pattern of a sunflower) in nature, and its recursive definition is here:

```
Fib(0) = 0
Fib(1) = 1
Fib(n) = Fib(n-1) + Fib(n-2) for n >= 2
```

Listing 4.12 displays the contents of `Fib.c` that illustrates how to calculate Fibonacci numbers.

LISTING 4.12: Fib.c

```
#include <stdio.h>

int fib(int num)
{
    if((num == 0)|| (num == 1))
    {
        return 1;
    }
    else
    {
        return fib(num-1)+fib(num-2);
    }
}

int main()
{
    int result=0, num=10;
    result = fib(num);

    printf("%d fibonacci = %d\n", num, result);

    return (0);
}
```

Listing 4.12 defines the fib() function with the parameter num. If num equals 0 or 1 then fib returns the value of num; otherwise, fib returns the result of adding fib(num-1) and fib(num-2). As you can see, the user-defined fib() function is precisely the implementation of the definition of Fibonacci numbers. The output from Listing 4.12 is here:

```
Fibonacci value of 10 = 89
```

CALCULATING THE POWER OF A NUMBER VIA RECURSION

Listing 4.13 displays the contents of ComputePower.c that uses recursion to calculate a number raised to a given power.

LISTING 4.13: ComputePower.c

```
#include <stdio.h>

long computePower(int b,int e, int r)
{
    if( e == 0 ) return r;
    computePower(b, e-1, r*b);
}

int main()
{
    int base = 4, exp = 5;
    long int result;

    result = computePower(base, exp, 1);
```

```
printf("%d to the power of %d = %ld\n",base, exp,
       result);

return 0;
}
```

Listing 4.13 defines the function `computePower()` with the parameters b, e, and r, that correspond to the base, exponent, and result, respectively. This function uses "tail recursion:" the intermediate results of the recursive calculations are passed as the third parameter. Each time the custom function `computePower()` is invoked, the third parameter is updated with a new intermediate product and the value of the exponent e is decremented. The terminating condition occurs when the value of e is 0, whereupon the value of the third parameter r is returned.

The output from Listing 4.13 is here:

```
4 to the power of 5 = 1024
```

CALCULATING THE NUMBER OF DIGITS OF A NUMBER VIA RECURSION

Listing 4.14 displays the contents of `CountDigits.c` that uses recursion to calculate the number of digits of a number.

LISTING 4.14: CountDigits.c

```
#include <stdio.h>

int countDigits(int num, int result)
{
    if( num == 0 ) return result;
    countDigits(num/10, result+1);
}

int main()
{
    int number = 123, result = 0;

    result = countDigits(number, 0);
    printf("Number of digits in %d = %d\n", number, result);

    return 0;
}
```

Listing 4.14 defines the custom function `countDigits()` that also uses *tail recursion* to calculate the number of digits in an integer. Notice that `countDigits()` is invoked by successively dividing the current number by 10, and simultaneously incrementing the value of the second parameter. The terminating condition occurs when the first parameter is 0, in which case the second parameter `result` equals the number of digits in the original number. The output from Listing 4.14 is here:

```
4 to the power of 5 = 1024
```

CALCULATING THE SUM OF THE DIGITS OF A NUMBER VIA RECURSION

Listing 4.15 displays the contents of `AddDigits.c` that uses recursion to calculate the sum of the digits of a number.

LISTING 4.15: AddDigits.c

```c
#include <stdio.h>

int computeSum(int num, int result)
{
    if( num == 0 ) return result;
    computeSum(num/10, result + num % 10);
}

int main()
{
    int number = 123, result = 0;

    result = computeSum(number, 0);
    printf("Sum of digits in %d = %d\n", number, result);

    return 0;
}
```

Listing 4.15 defines the function `computeSum()` that uses tail recursion to calculate the sum of two numbers. Notice that `countDigits()` is invoked by successively dividing the first parameter `num` by 10, and simultaneously adding the remainder `num % 10` to the second parameter. The terminating condition occurs when the first parameter is 0, in which case the second parameter `result` equals the sum of the two original numbers. The output from Listing 4.15 is here:

```
4 to the power of 5 = 1024
```

CALCULATING THE GCD OF TWO NUMBERS VIA RECURSION

The GCD (greatest common divisor) of two positive integers is the largest integer that divides both integers with a remainder of 0. Some values are shown here:

```
gcd(6,2)   = 2
gcd(10,4)  = 2
gcd(24,16) = 8
```

Listing 4.16 uses recursion and Euclid's algorithm in order to find the GCD of two positive integers. Keep in mind that although there is a more "compact" version of Euclid's algorithm, the code in Listing 4.17 is probably easier to understand.

LISTING 4.16: GCD.c

```c
#include <stdio.h>

int gcd(int num1, int num2)
{
    if(num1 % num2 == 0)
    {
        return num2;
    }
    else if(num1 < num2)
    {
        printf("switching %d and %d\n", num1, num2);
        return gcd(num2, num1);
    }
    else
    {
        printf("reducing %d and %d\n", num1, num2);
        return gcd(num1-num2, num2);
    }
}

int main()
{
    int result=0, num1=24, num2=10;
    result = gcd(num1, num2);

    printf("GCD of %d and %d = %d\n", num1, num2, result);

    return 0;
}
```

Listing 4.16 defines the function gcd with the parameters num1 and num2. If num1 is divisible by num2, the function returns num2. If num1 is less than num2, then gcd is invoked by switching the order of num1 and num2. In all other cases, gcd returns the result of computing gcd with the values num1-num2 and num2.

The output from Listing 4.16 is here:

```
reducing 24   and   10
reducing 14   and   10
switching 4   and   10
reducing 10   and   4
reducing  6   and   4
switching 2   and   4
GCD of    24  and 10 = 2
```

CALCULATING THE LCM OF TWO NUMBERS VIA RECURSION

The LCM (lowest common multiple) of two positive integers is the smallest integer that is a multiple of those two integers. Some values are shown here:

```
lcm(6,2)   = 2
lcm(10,4)  = 20
lcm(24,16) = 48
```

In general, if x and y are two positive integers, you can calculate their LCM as follows:

```
lcm(x,y) = x/gcd(x,y)*y/gcd(x.y)
```

Listing 4.17 uses the gcd() function that is defined in the previous section in order to calculate the LCM of two positive integers.

LISTING 4.17: LCM.c

```c
#include <stdio.h>

int gcd(int num1, int num2)
{
    if(num1 % num2 == 0)
    {
        return num2;
    }
    else if(num1 < num2)
    {
     //printf("switching %d and %d\n", num1, num2);
        return gcd(num2, num1);
    }
    else
    {
     //printf("reducing %d and %d\n", num1, num2);
        return gcd(num1-num2, num2);
    }
}

int main()
{
    int gcd1=0, lcm1=0, num1=24, num2=10;
    gcd1 = gcd(num1, num2);
    lcm1 = num1/gcd1*num2/gcd1;

    printf("LCM of %d and %d = %d\n", num1, num2, lcm1);

    return (0);
}
```

Listing 4.17 defines the function gcd that was discussed in the previous section, followed by the main() function. After initializing gcd1, lcm1, num1, and num2, the main() function invokes the gcd function that computes the GCD of num1 and num2. Next, the variable lcm1 is equal to num1/gcd1 multiplied by `num2/gcd1`, which is the LCM of `num1` and `num2`. The output of Listing 4.17 is here:

```
The LCM of 24 and 10 = 60
```

SUMMARY

This chapter introduced you some built-in functions in C, including string manipulation functions. You saw how to convert between data types, and how to print to a buffer. Then you learned how to work with error handling functions and buffer manipulation functions. Next you saw how to define custom function, how to specify function prototypes, and some commonly used header files.

You also learned how to pass an array as an argument to a function and how to calculate the transpose of a square matrix. In addition, you saw how to find a character in a string, how to pass by reference versus value. Then you learned about recursion, and how to calculate factorial values, Fibonacci numbers, the GCD of two numbers, and the LCM of two numbers. You also learned how to calculate the number of digits in an integer and how to calculate the sum of two numbers using a technique called tail recursion.

## CHAPTER 5

WORKING WITH POINTERS IN C

This chapter introduces pointers, which are often misunderstood and can be intimidating because of the conflicting and inaccurate explanation that you can find on the Internet.

Languages like Java have removed pointers entirely because of their complexity, and C requires that a block of code be marked unsafe in order to access pointers. On the other hand, pointers are used extensively in C, so a good foundation is required in order to become an effective C programmer.

The first part of this chapter introduces you to the concept of a pointer in C, along with examples of pointers to numbers, arrays, and strings. This section also contains C programs that use pointers to split a string and `for` loops that use pointers to find the divisors of a number.

The second part of this chapter defines pointers to arrays of numbers as well as pointers to functions. You will learn how to use pointers to reverse a string, find uppercase and lowercase letters, how to remove whitespaces from a string, and how to count words in a line of text. The final section of this chapter contains C programs that illustrate how to define pointers to functions, function pointers as arguments, and how to define pointers to pointers.

Now let's start with a brief introduction about pointers and pointer declarations, as well as the address of a variable, dereferencing pointers, and using pointer arithmetic. As you will see, pointer-based arithmetic emulates array indexing and the two views of an array as an indexed data structure or as a buffer with pointer arithmetic are crucial to the development and understanding of why C pointers work in the ways that they do.

WHAT ARE POINTERS?

A variable declared with a "pointer" data type contains a memory address indicating where the actual data is located. With pointer data types it is common to say that the pointer variable "points to" the actual data rather than talking about a memory address. Here are some examples of data that a pointer "points to:"

- a variable (such as int x = 5;)
- the starting address of a string (such as char *ptr = "Hello";)
- allocated via the built-in C malloc() function (discussed in Chapter 6)

Variables with a pointer data type are declared by placing an asterisk ("*") immediately before the name of a variable in a declaration. This variable may be used to point to any value of the appropriate type, or it can be set to NULL to indicate that it does not currently point to any value. Pointer can be declared for nearly any type of data, such as int, long, a user-defined struct (discussed in Chapter 6), or even a function. There is also a specific type of pointer: it has the syntax void * that is used to point to data whose type is not known.

A "pointer to a pointer" is defined with two asterisks ("**") and contains a memory address indicating where another pointer is located. One of the most common uses for pointer-to-a-pointer data types is simulating resizeable two-dimensional arrays.

The most important thing to be aware of when using pointers is that a pointer must always point to data of the appropriate type before it can used. Attempting to access a value "through" an invalid pointer is a common cause of failure and must be avoided.

There is another detail to keep in mind. When you assign a value to a pointer, the "thing on the right side of the equals sign" can be a hard-coded character string such as "Hello" (shown in the earlier list of examples). Why doesn't this violate the rule specified in the preceding paragraph? A quoted string (known as a "string literal") has a data type of "pointer to char." Since C has no built-in string data type, a string literal is treated as a pointer to its first character.

If you feel unsure of the meaning of the preceding paragraphs, the following subsections contain code examples that will make everything clear.

Simple Examples of Pointers

This section contains examples that reinforce the information in the previous section, with expanded explanations to reinforce the correct way to define pointers in C.

As you saw in the preceding section, a pointer in C is declared by putting an asterisk (*) in front of the variable name in the declaration statement, as shown here:

```
int *p;
```

The "*" operator *dereferences* a variable: this means that whenever you have a pointer to a memory location, use the "*" operator to obtain whatever is referenced by the pointer variable.

Note that the * character has multiple meanings. When it appears in a declaration, it acts as part of the data type to declare a pointer. When it appears in an expression to the left of a pointer it is the dereference operator, which accesses the data that the pointer currently points to. When it appears in an expression between two numeric values, it acts as the multiplication operator.

What if you want to access the value of a non-pointer variable? You can use the "&" operator to obtain the memory location of a non-pointer variable, after which you can access the value of that variable. For example, consider the following code snippet:

```
int x = 7;
int *p = &x;
```

As you can see, the variable x in the preceding code snippet has type int and has the value 7, whereas the variable p is a *pointer* to the memory address that is allocated for the variable x.

Notice the following: the pointer p has been initialized with the address of the variable x *after* the variable x has been declared *and* initialized with the value 7.

Another way to achieve the same result is shown in the following snippet:

```
int *p;
int x = 7;
p = &x;
```

In the preceding code snippet, p is declared as an uninitialized pointer to an integer, and then x is initialized as an integer whose value is 7, followed by setting the value of p equal to the address of x (which is denoted by &x).

Keep in mind that assigning values can only be done when data types match. For example, assigning int x = 7 is valid because the left and right side data types are both int.

As another example, declaring and assigning a pointer with int *p = &x is valid because the left and right side data types are both int *.

As a third example, the declaration int *p = 1234 is invalid because the left side has the type "pointer to int" and the right side has the type "int." Even if the types match, *you must also ensure the address assigned to a pointer is a valid address of data in your program.* Based on the preceding statement, we know that the code snippet int *p=1234 is invalid because of a type error.

On the other hand, the following code snippet *is* valid because the pointer p is initialized with the address of the variable x that is declared *before* the pointer p is declared and initialized:

```
int x = 7;
int *p = &x;
```

The reason for the restriction is that pointers may only be used to access other data in your program. The compiler is allowed to assume that your program is correct and pointers always refer to valid data. The compiler is allowed to optimize your code based on this assumption; if you violate this rule then your program may crash.

Another point to keep in mind: using a pointer allows you to modify the data it points to by altering the contents of the given memory address. Here is an example:

```
// x is initially 7
int x = 7;

// p points to the location of x
int *p = &x;

// update the contents of x via p
*p = 1234;

// x is now equal to 1234!
```

const Pointers

A constant pointer, sometimes referred to as "pointer to const," is a pointer which cannot be used to modify the data it points to, an example of which is here:

```
const char *name_ptr = "Test";
```

If we put the const after the *, then the meaning of the const changes. If the declaration begins with "char * const" then the pointer can never be modified to point to a different location, but it can be used to modify the character it points to.

Finally, put const in both places to create a pointer that cannot be modified to a data item that cannot be changed, as shown here:

```
const char *const title_ptr = "Title";
```

POINTERS TO INTEGER VARIABLES

Listing 5.1 displays the contents of SimplePointer1.c that illustrates how to use a pointer to change the value of a variable of type int. Make sure that you have read the previous section in order to make sense of the code in this section. Although you saw the first portion of Listing 5.1 earlier in this chapter, it's repeated here to provide additional reinforcement.

LISTING 5.1: SimplePointer1.c

```
#include <stdio.h>

int main()
{
    int x = 7;
    printf("Value of x:    %d\n", x);
```

```
// ptr "points" to location of x:
int *ptr = &x;
*ptr = 45;
printf("Value of x:    %d\n", x);

// update value of x to 1234;
*(&x) = 1234;
printf("Value of x:    %d\n", x);

// error: cannot assign x to an explicit address
// &x = 1234;

return 0;
}
```

Listing 5.1 contains the same code that you saw earlier in this chapter, this time in a complete C program. Once again notice the comment near the end of Listing 5.1 that explains why the assignment statement is invalid.

The output from Listing 5.1 is here:

```
Value of x:    7
Value of x:    45
Value of x:    1234
```

Let's expand the preceding code sample with some other examples of pointers. Listing 5.2 displays the contents of SimplePointer2.c that illustrates how to use a pointer to change the value of a non-pointer variable of type int.

LISTING 5.2: SimplePointer2.c

```
#include <stdio.h>

int main()
{
    int x = 7;
    printf("Value of x:    %d\n", x);

    // ptr "points" to location of x:
    int *ptr = &x;

    // ptr2 points to same location as ptr:
    int *ptr2 = ptr;

    // update value of x:
    *ptr2  = 5678;

    printf("Value of x:    %d\n", x);
    printf("Value of ptr:  %d\n", *ptr2);
    printf("Value of ptr2: %d\n", *ptr2);

    return 0;
}
```

Listing 5.2 contains the variable x whose initial value is 7, followed by the pointer ptr that is the same as the pointer ptr in Listing 5.2. Next, the pointer ptr2 is initialized with the location of pointer ptr, after which the contents of ptr2 are changed to 5678. The result is probably what you expect: the new value of the variable is 5678. The output from Listing 5.2 is here:

```
Value of x:    7
Value of x:    5678
Value of ptr:  5678
Value of ptr2: 5678
```

Listing 5.3 displays the contents of SimplePointer3.c that illustrates how to use a pointer to change the value of a variable of type int.

LISTING 5.3: SimplePointer3.c

```c
#include <stdio.h>

int main()
{
   int x = 7;
   printf("Value of x:    %d\n", x);

   // ptr "points" to location of x:
   int *ptr = &x;
   printf("Value of ptr:  %d\n", *ptr);

   // ptr2 points to same location as ptr:
   int *ptr2 = ptr;
   printf("Value of ptr2: %d\n", *ptr2);

   // the address of ptr2 plus one:
   int *ptr3 = ptr2+1;
   printf("Value of ptr3: %d\n", *ptr3);

   // uncomment this block to see the error message:
 //int *ptr4 = *ptr2+1;
 //printf("Value of ptr4: %d\n", *ptr4);

   return 0;
}
```

The first portion of Listing 5.3 is the same as Listing 5.2, followed by the pointer ptr3 that is initialized with the value of the expression ptr2+1. There are two possibilities: either the preceding expression equals the contents of ptr2 plus 1 (which equals 8), or the preceding expression equals the memory address of ptr2 plus 1. If you chose the latter, you chose the correct answer! The output from Listing 5.3 is here:

```
Value of x:    7
Value of ptr:  7
Value of ptr2: 7
Value of ptr3: 1406395048
```

MULTIPLE POINTERS AND INTEGER VARIABLES

Listing 5.4 displays the contents of `PointersNumbers1.c` that illustrates how to combine integers and pointers in a C program.

LISTING 5.4: PointersNumbers1.c

```
#include <stdio.h>

int main()
{
    int x=3, y=5;
    int *ptr;

    printf("x = %d\n", x);
    printf("y = %d\n", y);

    ptr = &x;
    *ptr = 7;

    ptr = &y;
    *ptr = 23;

    printf("x = %d\n", x);
    printf("y = %d\n", y);
}
```

Listing 5.4 contains two integer variables x and y whose values are 3 and 5, respectively. Next, the pointer ptr is assigned the memory location of the variable x, after which the value at that location is changed to 7.

Next, the pointer ptr is assigned the memory location of the variable y, after which the value at that address is changed to 23. The output from Listing 5.4 is here:

```
x = 3
y = 5
x = 7
y = 23
```

POINTERS AND CHARACTER STRINGS

Until this point in the chapter, you have seen various examples of pointers and integer-valued variables. You can also assign pointers to memory locations that are occupied by character strings (such as "John Smith"). Examples involving pointers and C structures appear later in this chapter and in the next chapter.

C pointers to character strings can be expressed in several ways, all of which achieve the same result. When you are defining C pointers, remember that you must specify the data type because there is no restriction on the contents of a memory location: it can be the starting address of a standard C data type or a custom data structure (discussed in Chapter 6). Hence, a pointer needs information about the type of data at a memory location (int, char, and so forth).

Listing 5.5 displays the contents of SimpleString.c that illustrates various ways of assigning pointers to a character string.

LISTING 5.5: SimpleString.c

```
#include <stdio.h>

int main()
{
    char *str   = "thisisalongstring";

    char *ptr1 = (char *)&str;       // incorrect
    char *ptr2 = (char *)&str[0];
    char *ptr3 = &str[0];
    char *ptr4 = str;
  //char *ptr5 = &str;               // warning

    printf("str:   %s\n", str);
  //printf("ptr1: %s\n", ptr1);
    printf("ptr2: %s\n", ptr2);
    printf("ptr3: %s\n", ptr3);
    printf("ptr4: %s\n", ptr4);
  //printf("ptr5: %s\n", ptr5);

    return 0;
}
```

Let's look at each of the pointer declarations in Listing 5.5, one at a time, to see their similarities and their differences. If you need to read the following description more than once, that's perfectly fine (after all, the concept of pointers in C is new to you).

Listing 5.5 starts by initializing the pointer str to the location of the hardcoded string thisisalongstring. Next, the variables ptr1 and ptr5 point to the address of the variable str, whereas ptr2, ptr3, and ptr4 point to the first character in the string literal.

The declaration of ptr1 causes it to point to the variable str, which is invalid because str is not a character but a character pointer. The type cast on this line prevents the compiler from warning about the type mismatch.

The initializer for ptr2 can be read as "get the first character in the string str points to, then take its address, and then cast it to "char *" which is valid but a bit cumbersome. The cast is unnecessary because the data type already is char *, and the address of the first character is the same as the value already stored in str.

The declaration for ptr3 has the same effect as ptr2 but omits the unnecessary cast, and the declaration for ptr4 also omits the address of and indexing operations.

As tempting as it might be, the syntax for ptr5 produces the following compilation warning:

```
SimpleString.c:10:17: warning: initialization from
incompatible pointer type [-Wincompatible-pointer-types]
    char *ptr5 = &str; // warning
              ^
```

The next portion of Listing 5.5 contains six printf() statements that print the values of the contents of the six pointers. The output from Listing 5.5 is here:

```
str:  thisisalongstring
ptr2: thisisalongstring
ptr3: thisisalongstring
ptr4: thisisalongstring
```

Use the syntax for ptr2, ptr3, or ptr4 (ptr4 has the simplest syntax) when you define a pointer to a character string, and be consistent in your coding convention.

DISPLAYING SUBSTRINGS OF A STRING

The example in this section is mainly for fun, yet it's useful because it shows you how to "walk" a pointer through a character string and display partial strings, all of which is performed in a nested loop.

Listing 5.6 displays the contents of Substrings.c that illustrates how to display substrings of a given string.

LISTING 5.6: Substrings.c

```c
#include <stdio.h>

int main()
{
    char *str = "thisisalongstring";
    int len = strlen(str);

    for(int i=1; i<=len; i++)
    {
        printf("%2d: ",i);
        for(int j=0; j<i; j++)
        {
            printf("%c", (char)str[j]);
        }
        printf("\n");
    }
}
```

Listing 5.6 starts with a character-based pointer str that points to a string of characters. Recall the discussion about character strings earlier in this chapter: assigning the dereferenced value of a pointer to a character string is a legitimate way to initialize a character pointer.

The next part of Listing 5.6 contains a pair of nested loops. As the outer loop iterates through each of the characters in the string referenced by str, the inner loop iterates through all the characters in the string `str` that precede (and include) the current character.

Listing 5.6 introduces the C built-in function `strlen()` that returns the length of a string. The output from Listing 5.6 is here:

```
 1: t
 2: th
 3: thi
 4: this
 5: thisi
 6: thisis
 7: thisisa
 8: thisisal
 9: thisisalo
10: thisisalon
11: thisisalong
12: thisisalongs
13: thisisalongst
14: thisisalongstr
15: thisisalongstri
16: thisisalongstrin
17: thisisalongstring
```

DISPLAY COMMAND LINE ARGUMENTS IN C

You can determine the number of arguments (and their string-based values) that are specified as command line arguments to a C program, with the following modified syntax for the `main()` function:

```
int main(int argc, char *argv[])
```

The argument `argc` is the number of command arguments whereas `argv` is a pointer to an array that contains the actual arguments that are specified at the command line. As you can see, there's a slight "twist" with the second argument in the `main()` method: `char **argv`, which is actually the same as `char *argv[]`. We'll use the latter syntax because it's conceptually easier (i.e., a pointer to an array of strings).

Listing 5.7 displays the contents of `PrintCmdLineArgs.c` that illustrates how to print the command line arguments of a C program.

LISTING 5.7: PrintCmdLineArgs.c

```c
#include <stdio.h>

int main(int argc, char *argv[])
{
    int i;

    printf("Display Command Line Arguments\n");
    for( i = 0; i < argc; ++i )
    {
        printf("Argument %d = \"%s\"\n", i, argv[i]);
    }
```

```
    return 0;
}
```

Listing 5.7 contains a loop that iterates through the command line arguments and prints them via the `printf()` function. After compiling the code, launch the program in Listing 5.7 as follows (you can use different arguments):

```
./PrintCmdLineArguments 1 a 2 b 3 c
```

The output is here:

```
Display Command Line Arguments
Argument 0 = "./PrintCmdLineArguments"
Argument 1 = "1"
Argument 2 = "a"
Argument 3 = "2"
Argument 4 = "b"
Argument 5 = "3"
Argument 6 = "c"
```

You can easily check for the number of arguments and perform an early exit with the `exit()` function, as shown in the following code block:

```
#include <stdio.h>
#include <stdlib.h> // required for the exit() function

int main(int argc, char *argv[])
{
   if( argc < 3 )
   {
      fprintf(stderr, "Not enough Arguments: %d\n", argc);
      exit(-1);
   }

   // proceed normally...
}
```

Although you can perform an early exit with the `abort()` function, keep in mind that the latter does not flush buffers of open files. Moreover, the `abort()` function on a Unix system results in a core dump.

INCREMENTING POINTERS: MEMORY LOCATION VERSUS VALUE

C supports pointer arithmetic (i.e., addition and subtraction). You need to understand the difference between adding (incrementing) a pointer *location* and adding (incrementing) the *value* of a pointer. In fact, we already saw an example of accessing the location of a pointer in Listing 5.2.

In other to illustrate this difference, consider the following code snippet:

```
char array[5];
char *array_ptr = &array[0];
```

In the preceding code snippet, `*array_ptr` is the same as `array[0]`, and `*(array_ptr+1)` is the same as `array[1]`, and `*(array_ptr+2)` is the same as `array[1]`, and so on. Note the use of parentheses.

However, `(*array_ptr)+1` is *not* the same as `array[1]`, because the +1 is *outside* the parentheses, which means that it is added *after* the dereference. Consequently, the expression `(*array_ptr)+1` is the same as `array[0]+1`. Recall that an array consists of a block of consecutive memory locations, each of which holds an element of the array. For example, if the array `myarr` starts from the memory location `0xff001320`, then `myarr[0]` has the same address, whereas `myarr` occupies the memory location that—in the case of an integer—is 4 bytes beyond this location: `0xff001324` (for a double it would be `8 bytes`). When you define a pointer, you specify the data type for the pointer, and therefore incrementing a pointer will increment the memory location by the number of bytes associated with the data type: one byte for a character, 4 bytes for integers, and 8 bytes for double.

Listing 5.8 displays the contents of `ArrayAndPointer1.c` that illustrates how to print the elements (and their addresses) of a simple character array.

LISTING 5.8: ArrayAndPointer1.c

```
#include <stdio.h>

int main()
{
    int numbers[5] = {2, 3, 5, 7, 11};
    printf("First item in numbers  = %i\n", *numbers);

    int *numbers2 = &numbers[1];
    printf("First item in numbers2 = %i\n", numbers2[0]);

    return 0;
}
```

Listing 5.8 defines the array `numbers` that contains five integers, followed a `printf()` statement that displays the first number in the `numbers` array. Notice the use of `*numbers2` to point to the first element in the `numbers` array.

Next, Listing 5.8 defines the pointer `numbers2` that is initialized with the memory location of the *second* number in the array `numbers`.

Compile the code in Listing 5.8 and launch the executable and you will see the following output:

```
First item in numbers  = 2
First item in numbers2 = 3
```

POINTERS AND ARRAYS

Listing 5.9 displays the contents of `PointersToNumbers1.c` that illustrates how to use an index in order to iterate through the elements of an array, and illustrates a coding style that is better to avoid in your own code.

LISTING 5.9: *PointersToNumbers1.c*

```c
#include <stdio.h>

int array[] = {4, 5, 8, 9, 8, 1, 0, 1, 9, 3};

int main()
{
   int index;
   while (array[index] != 0)
     ++index;

   printf("Number of elements before 9: %d\n", index);

   return (0);
}
```

Listing 5.9 starts with the definition of the global variable array that is initialized with 10 integers. The main() function contains a while loop that iterates through the elements of array and also increments the variable index during each iteration. The while loop exists when the value 0 is encountered, and then the value of index is displayed. The output from launching the code is here:

```
Number of elements before 9: 6
```

The point to observe is that the following syntax is concise and yet can be misread (especially by novices):

```c
while (array[index] != 0)
   ++index;
```

You might think that the preceding while loop is "stuck" in an infinite loop because the value of the variable index *is never incremented*. In fact, the statement ++index; is "attached" to the while loop, and eventually the loop will terminate.

The following code snippet is equivalent to the preceding code snippet. However, the syntax is explicit and emphasizes the fact that the variable index is incremented during each iteration in the while loop:

```c
while (array[index] != 0)
{
   ++index;
}
```

The preceding code block is 100% unambiguous (even to a novice). Another advantage of the preceding code snippet is that you can easily add more code inside the curly braces without accidentally forgetting to include the existing ++index; statement.

POINTERS, ARRAYS, AND ADDRESSES

Listing 5.10 displays the contents of `PointersToNumbers2.c` that illustrates how to print the elements (and their addresses) of a simple character array.

LISTING 5.10: PointersNumbers2.c

```
#include <stdio.h>

#define ARRAY_SIZE 10
char array[ARRAY_SIZE + 1] = "0123456789";

int main()
{
  int index;
  printf("&array[index] (array+index) array[index]\n");

  for(index=0; index < ARRAY_SIZE; ++index) {
    printf("0x%-10p 0x%-10p 0x%x\n",
           &array[index],(array+index),array[index]);
  }

  return 0;
}
```

Listing 5.10 starts with the `#define` directive (a preprocessor directive that performs text substitution) that sets `ARRAY_SIZE` to the value 10. The next code snippet defines the character-based variable array that is initialized with 10 digits, which are treated as characters.

Recall that characters occupy one byte, and therefore consecutive array elements occupy consecutive memory addresses. Next, a short `int` occupies two bytes, which means the memory addresses of consecutive array elements increase by two (not by one).

Moreover, C will automatically perform the correct pointer arithmetic (i.e., increment by the correct number). Hence, the expression `array+1` is interpreted correctly: it refers to the element with index 1 (i.e., the second element in the array). In other words, `array+1` increments the value of the *index* by 1 and does *not* increment the address value by 1. As a result, the following code snippets are equivalent:

```
array_ptr = &array[0];
array_ptr = array;
```

The output from Listing 5.10 is here:

```
&array[index] (array+index) array[index]
0x0x1033e3020 0x0x1033e3020 0x30
0x0x1033e3021 0x0x1033e3021 0x31
0x0x1033e3022 0x0x1033e3022 0x32
0x0x1033e3023 0x0x1033e3023 0x33
```

```
0x0x1033e3024 0x0x1033e3024 0x34
0x0x1033e3025 0x0x1033e3025 0x35
0x0x1033e3026 0x0x1033e3026 0x36
0x0x1033e3027 0x0x1033e3027 0x37
0x0x1033e3028 0x0x1033e3028 0x38
0x0x1033e3029 0x0x1033e3029 0x39
```

POINTER ARITHMETIC

C "blurs" the distinction between pointers and arrays by treating them in the same manner in many cases (recall that char **argv and char *argv[] are the same). In this section the code uses the variable array_ptr as a pointer, and C automatically does the necessary conversion.

Listing 5.11 displays the contents of PointerArithmetic.c that illustrates how to perform pointer arithmetic in order to iterate through the elements of the same array as Listing 5.10.

LISTING 5.11: PointerArithmetic.c

```
#include <stdio.h>

int arr[] = {4, 5, 8, 9, 8, 1, 0, 1, 9, 3};

int main()
{
   int *arr_ptr = arr;

   while ((*arr_ptr) != 0) ++arr_ptr;

   printf("Number of elements before 9: %d\n", arr_ptr -
arr);

   return (0);
}
```

Notice that when we wish to examine the data in the array, we use the dereference operator (*). This operator is used in the statement:

```
while ((*arr_ptr) != 0)
```

When we wish to change the pointer itself, no other operator is used. For example, the following code snippet increments the pointer (not the data):

```
++arr_ptr;
```

Once again, we have an example of a coding style that has a more explicit alternative:

```
while ((*arr_ptr) != 0) ++arr_ptr;
```

Consider using the following alternative syntax, which involves only a few more keystrokes and is potentially less error-prone:

```
while ((*arr_ptr) != 0)
{
  ++arr_ptr;
}
```

CALCULATING THE TRANSPOSE OF A SQUARE MATRIX

In Chapter 2, you learned that the transpose of a square matrix is the result of interchanging the matrix elements by interchanging the row and column position. In other words, if the value of the element in the (i,j) position of matrix A is a(i,j), then the value of the element in the (i,j) position of the transpose of matrix A is a(j,i).

Listing 5.12 displays the contents of Transpose.c that illustrates how to calculate the transpose of a square matrix, and how to use one function to display the contents of the matrix before and after calculating its transpose.

LISTING 5.12: Transpose.c

```
#include <stdio.h>

void ptrArray(int *arr, int row, int col)
{
    for(int i=0; i<row; i++)
    {
        printf("Row %d: ",i);
        for(int j=0; j<col; j++)
        {
            printf("%d ", *(arr+i*row+j));
        }
        printf("\n");
    }
}

int main()
{
    int row=3, col=3, temp=0;
    int arr1[3]= {{1,2,3}, {4,5,6}, {7,8,9}};

    // display original matrix
    printf("Original\n");
    ptrArray(&arr1[0][0], row, col);

    for(int i=1; i<row; i++)
    {
        for(int j=0; j<i; j++)
        {
            temp = arr1[i][j];
            arr1[i][j] = arr1[j][i];
            arr1[j][i] = temp;
        }
    }

    // display transposed matrix
```

```
    printf("Transpose\n");
    ptrArray(&arr1[0][0], col, row);

    return 0;
}
```

Listing 5.12 starts with the user-defined function `ptrArray()` that displays the contents of an array. This function has three arguments: the first is a pointer to an array, the second is the number of rows in the array, and the third is the number of columns in the array. The function `ptrArray()` contains a nested loop that iterates through the rows and columns of the array and displays the values at each location.

Next, the function `main()` initializes some scalar variables as well as the array `arr1` that contains integer values. The next section of `main()` contains a nested loop that uses the temporary variable `temp` in order to "swap" the array entries `arr1[i][j]` and `arr1[j][i]`, after which the entries in `arr1` are the transpose of the original values.

The bottom section of `main()` invokes the function `ptrArray()` to display the contents of the transposed matrix. Notice that the variables `row` and `col` are reversed (as shown in bold): if A is an mxn matrix then the transpose of A is an nxm matrix. The output from Listing 5.12 is here:

```
Original
Row 0: 1 2 3
Row 1: 4 5 6
Row 2: 7 8 9
Transpose
Row 0: 1 4 7
Row 1: 2 5 8
Row 2: 3 6 9
```

As you can see, Listing 5.12 contains two identical blocks of code: a better solution is to use a function (discussed in Chapter 3) that prints the contents of an array.

POINTERS AND STRINGS

Listing 5.13 displays the contents of `PointersStrings1.c` that illustrates how to initialize strings and pointers.

LISTING 5.13: PointersStrings1.c

```
#include <stdio.h>

int main()
{
    char *ptr1   = "Hello World";
    char str1[]  = "Hello World";
    char *ptr2   = str1;

    printf("%s\n", ptr1);
```

```
    printf("%s\n", str1);
    printf("%s\n", ptr2);

    return 0;
}
```

Listing 5.13 contains a main() function that defines the three variables ptr1, str1, and ptr2 that consist of a pointer to a string, a string array of characters, and a pointer to the string array, respectively.

The second portion of the main() function contains three printf() statements that display the contents of the three variables (which are all the same).

Keep in mind that the following causes an error:

```
char[] str2 = "Hello World";
```

The output from executing the code in Listing 5.12 is here:

```
Hello World
Hello World
Hello World
```

POINTERS AND BUILT-IN STRING MANIPULATION FUNCTIONS

C supports a nice variety of built-in string manipulation functions. The following list is sort of a "dump" of C functions that provide such functionality, along with a terse description of their purpose (which is fairly evident from their names).

Copy src string into dest string with the strcpy() function:

```
char *strcpy (char *dest, char *src);
```

Copy the first n characters of string2 to string1 with the strncpy() function:

```
char *strncpy(char *string1, char *string2, int n);
```

Compare string1 and string2 to determine alphabetic order with the strcmp() function:

```
int strcmp(char *string1, char *string2);
```

Compare first n characters of two strings with the strncmp() function:

```
int strncmp(char *string1, char *string2, int n);
```

Determine the length of a string with the strlen() function:

```
int strlen(char *string);
```

Concatenate string src to the string dest with the strcat() function:

```
char *strcat(char *dest, const char *src);
```

Concatenate n characters from string `src` to the string `dest` with the `strncat()` function:

```
char *strncat(char *dest, const char *src, int n);
```

Find first occurrence of character c in string with the `strchr()` function:

```
char *strchr(char *string, int c);
```

Find last occurrence of character c in string with the `strrchr()` function:

```
char *strrchr(char *string, int c);
```

Find first occurrence of string `string1` in `string2` with the `strstr()` function:

```
char *strstr(char *string2, char *string1);
```

Parse the string s into tokens using `delim` as delimiter with the `strtok()` function:

```
char *strtok(char *s, const char *delim) ;
```

If you need a code sample that uses one of the preceding functions, but it's not available in this book, perform an online search and you will probably find several examples.

WHILE LOOPS AND POINTERS TO STRINGS

Listing 5.14 displays the contents of `WhileLoopStr.c` that shows you how to use a `while` loop in a C program.

LISTING 5.14: ForLoopStr.c

```c
#include <stdio.h>
#include <string.h>

int main()
{
    char *str = "hello";
    char *p = str;
    int i=0;
    int len = strlen(str);

    printf("First Loop\n");
    printf("----------\n");
    while(i<len)
    {
        printf("str[i] : %c\n", str[i]);
        ++i;
```

```
    }

    printf("\nSecond Loop\n");
    printf("-----------\n");
    while(*p)
    {
        printf("p : %s\n", p);
        ++p;
    }

    return 0;
}
```

Listing 5.14 contains a main() function that defines the variables ptr and p that are pointers to a string, and also the variable len that is the length of the string str.

Next, the main() function contains a loop that iterates through the characters in the string that is referenced by the variable str. The main() function contains a second loop that iterates through the same set of characters, but this time it's performed by advancing the location of the pointer p. The output from Listing 5.14 is here:

```
First Loop
----------
i : h
i : e
i : l
i : l
i : o

Second Loop
----------
char : hello
char : ello
char : llo
char : lo
char : o
```

If you replace while(*p) with the statement while(p), what do you think will happen? If your answer is "infinite loop" in the second while loop, you are correct. The reason is simple: while(p) always evaluates to true because p has a non-null address, whereas while(*p) evaluates to false when the pointer p reaches the end of the string str. Keep this detail in mind when you use pointer arithmetic.

COUNTING VOWELS AND CONSONANTS IN A TEXT STRING

The strchr() function locates the first occurrence of a character in a text string. Listing 5.15 displays the contents of CountVowelsConsonants.c that illustrates how to count the number of vowels, consonants, and other characters in a text string.

LISTING 5.15: CountVowelsConsonants.c

```c
#include <stdio.h>
#include <stdlib.h>
#include <string.h>
#include <ctype.h>

int charType(char ch)
{
  char ch2 = tolower(ch);

  if(ch2 =='a' || ch2 =='e' || ch2 =='i' || ch2 =='o' ||
ch2 =='u')
  {
    return 0;
  }
  else if(isalpha(ch2))
  {
    return 1;
  }
  else if(isdigit(ch2))
  {
    return 2;
  }
  else
  {
    return 3;
  }
}

int main()
{
    char str[] = "This is a string with some short words 1
2 3 4 that wraps around and let's see how well the code in
this code sample actually works!";

    char *ptr = str;

    int result, counts[4];
    counts[0] = counts[1] = counts[2] = counts= 0;

    while(*ptr)
    {
       result = charType(*ptr);
       ++counts[result];
       ptr++;
    }

    printf("VOWELS:    %d\n",counts[0]);
    printf("CONSONANT: %d\n",counts[1]);
    printf("DIGITS:    %d\n",counts[2]);
    printf("OTHERS:    %d\n",counts[3]);

    return 0;
}
```

Listing 5.15 starts with the definition of the function charType() that takes a character as a parameter and has a return type of int. This function contains conditional logic to determine whether the parameter ch is a vowel (by checking for the presence of each vowel individually), an alphabetic character (with the isalpha() built-in C function), a digit (with the isdigit() built-in C function), or some other character. The returned value is an integer between 0 and 3 inclusive, depending on which portion of the conditional logic is executed. Later in this section you will see the rationale for specifying these return values.

The next portion of Listing 5.15 is the main() function that initializes the character array str with a hard-coded string, followed by the character pointer ptr that is initialized with the location of the variable str. The counts array has four integer values, all of which are initially 0.

The next portion of Listing 5.15 is a loop that uses the pointer ptr to iterate through each character of the variable str. During each iteration, the current character is passed to the charType() function, and the return value is used to increment the corresponding position in the counts array. The position of ptr is incremented by one and the while() executes again, until we reach the end of the hard-coded string.

The output from Listing 5.15 is here:

```
First Loop
VOWELS:     33
CONSONANT: 66
DIGITS:     4
OTHERS:     25
```

FINDING A WORD IN A TEXT STRING IN C

The strchr() function locates the first occurrence of a character in a text string. Listing 5.16 displays the contents of FindChar1.c that illustrates how to find a character in a text string.

LISTING 5.16: FindChar1.c

```c
#include <stdio.h>
#include <string.h>

#define SIZE 80

int main(void)
{
    char line[SIZE] = "New York Pizza";
    char *ptr;
    int ch = 'z';

    ptr = strchr(line, ch);
    printf("The first occurrence of %c in '%s' is '%s'\n",
           ch, line, ptr);
```

```
    return 0;
}
```

Listing 5.16 starts by initializing the character string `line` with a hard-coded string, followed by declaring the character pointer `ptr` and initializing the integer-valued variable `ch` with "z."

Next, `ptr` is assigned the value that is returned from invoking the built-in C function `strchr()` with the arguments `line` and `ch`. As you saw earlier in this chapter, this function returns the first occurrence of the character assigned to the argument `ch`.

The output from launching the code in Listing 5.16 is here:

```
The first occurrence of z in 'New York Pizza' is 'zza'
```

SEARCHING A WORD IN A TEXT STRING IN C

The `strstr()` function locates the first occurrence of the null-terminated string s2 in the null-terminated string s1. The `strcasestr()` function is similar to `strstr()`, but ignores the case of both strings. The latter function is not part of standard C; however, it is a common (but not universal) vendor extension.

Listing 5.17 displays the contents of `SearchForWordInString.c` that illustrates how to tokenize a text string into words.

LISTING 5.17: SearchForWordInString.c

```
#include <stdio.h>
#include <string.h>

int main()
{
    char *str = "One two Three four";
    char *word1 = "our";
    char *word2 = "three";

    if((strstr(str, word1)) != NULL)
    {
        printf("Current Line: %s\n", str);
        printf("Exact Match:  %s\n\n", word1);
    }

    return 0;
}
```

Listing 5.17 starts by initializing the character string `str` with a hard-coded string, followed by initializing the character pointers `word1` and `word2` with the strings `our` and `three`, respectively.

Next, the code contains a conditional block that invokes the built-in C function `strstr()` to check for the presence of word in `str1`, and if a match is found, an appropriate message is displayed. The output from launching the code in Listing 5.17 is here:

```
Current Line: One two Three four
Exact Match:  our
```

CONCATENATING TWO STRINGS IN C

Listing 5.18 displays the contents of ConcatenateStrings.c that illustrates how to use the strcat() and strncat() functions in order to concatenate two strings. Keep in mind the following distinction: the strcat() function appends the second string to the first string, whereas the strncat() function appends only the specified number of characters in the second string to the first string.

LISTING 5.18: ConcatenateStrings.c

```c
#include <stdio.h>
#include <string.h>

#define BUFFER_SIZE 80

int main()
{
  char line[BUFFER_SIZE] = "New York";
  char *ptr;

  // Call strcat with line and " pizza"
  ptr = strcat(line, " pizza" );
  printf("strcat line  = %s\n", line);

  // Reset line to contain the original string
  memset(line, '\0', sizeof(line));
  ptr = strcpy(line, "New York");
  strcpy(line, "New York");

  // Call strncat with line and two chars of "pizza"
  ptr = strncat(line, " pizza", 3);
  printf("strncat line = %s\n", line);

  return 0;
}
```

Listing 5.18 starts by defining BUFFER_SIZE with the value 90 (you will see more about the #define preprocessor directive in Chapter 7). Next, the main() function initializes the character string line with a hard-coded string, followed by declaring the character pointer ptr.

The next portion of Listing 5.18 initializes ptr with the value that is returned from invoking the built-in C function strcat() with the parameters line and the string "pizza," after which the new contents of line are displayed.

The next portion of Listing 5.18 initializes ptr with the value that is returned from invoking the built-in C function strncat() with the parameters line and the string "New York," after which the new contents of line are displayed. The final section of code involves a second invocation of the strncat() function, along with displaying the result.

The output from Listing 5.18 is here:

```
strcat line  = New York pizza
strncat line = New York pi
```

SUMMARY

This chapter introduced you to the concept of a pointer in C, along with examples of pointers to numbers, arrays, and strings. You saw how to use pointers to split a string, as well as for loops that use pointers to find the divisors of a number. Next, you learned how to define pointers to arrays of numbers as well as pointers to functions.

You also learned how to use pointers to reverse a string, find uppercase and lowercase letters, and how to remove whitespaces from a string. Then you saw how to count words in a line of text, as well as work with words and strings in while loops. Finally, you saw an example of counting vowels and consonants in a string, and how to concatenate two strings.

## CHAPTER 6

WORKING WITH POINTERS

This chapter continues the discussion of C pointers that began in Chapter 5 and contains code samples that illustrate slightly more complex ways to use pointers in C programs. After you complete this chapter, you will be in a good position to understand the section in Chapter 7 that shows you how to use pointers in conjunction with C structs.

The first part of this chapter contains code samples that illustrate how to compare two strings and how to "tokenize" the words in a text string, and how to check if a string is a palindrome.

The second part of this chapter introduces you to some built-in C functions that allocate memory dynamically, along with a C function that frees that allocated memory when it is no longer needed (which avoids memory leaks). This section also contains pointer-based code samples for iterating through an array of numbers, converting strings to uppercase or lowercase letters, and how to find the prime divisors of a positive integer.

The final section of this chapter contains C programs that illustrate how to define pointers to functions, function pointers as arguments, pointers to pointers, and how to process command line arguments.

Although this chapter will not make you an expert in C pointers, you will be able to understand many C programs that contain pointers, how to define your own pointer-based functions, and be able to recognize many ways in which pointers can be used in C programs.

COMPARING TWO STRINGS IN C

The `strcmp()` function is a built-in C function that enables you to compare to two strings. Listing 6.1 displays the contents of `CompareStrings.c` that illustrates how to use the `strcmp()` function.

LISTING 6.1: CompareStrings.c

```c
#include <stdio.h>
#include <string.h>

int main()
{
    char *str1 = "abc";
    char *str2 = "abcd";

    int num = strcmp(str1, str2);

    printf("String1: %s\n", str1);
    printf("String2: %s\n", str2);

    if(strcmp(str1, str2) == 0 )
    {
        printf("Strings are equal: %s %s\n", str1, str2);
    }
    else if(strcmp(str1, str2) < 0 )
    {
        printf("First < second:    %s %s\n", str1, str2);
    }
    else
    {
        printf("First > second:    %s %s\n", str1, str2);
    }

    return 0;
}
```

Listing 6.1 contains the `main()` function that initializes the character pointers `str1` and `str2`. Next, the value of the integer `num` is initialized by invoking the `strcmp()` function with the arguments `str1` and `str2`.

The next portion of the `main()` function contains conditional logic that displays a message based on whether the value of the `strcmp()` function is 0, negative, or positive. The output is here:

```
String1: abc
String2: abcd
First < second:    abc abcd
```

In addition, there is also the built-in C function `strnicmp()` that performs a case-insensitive comparison of two strings, as shown here:

```
result = strnicmp(str1, str2, 8);
```

The conditional logic for `strnicmp()` is the same as the conditional logic for `strcmp()` in Listing 5.18 in Chapter 5.

NOTE *The* `strnicmp()` *function is a vendor extension, not part of the C standard.*

USING STRTOK() TO TOKENIZE A STRING

Consider the case of a string that has the form "Last/First", such as "Smith/John". The task is to split such a string into two separate strings: the string on the left side of the "/" symbol and the string on the right side of the "/" symbol. We can perform this task via the built-in C function strtok().

The strtok() function takes a pointer to a string (string_ptr) and a character to find (such as "/") as its arguments. Next, we employ a while loop that finds subsequent tokens in the remaining string.

Listing 6.2 displays the contents of Tokenize.c that illustrates how to split a string into tokens (i.e., individual words).

LISTING 6.2: Tokenize.c

```c
#include <stdio.h>
#include <string.h>

char *delim = "/";

void tokenizeString(char *str)
{
   // first token = last name
   char *token = strtok(str, delim);
   char *second = token;
   char *first;
   int count = 0;

   // print token after delimiter
   while (token != NULL)
   {
      token = strtok(NULL, delim);
      first = token;
   }

   printf("NAME: %s %s\n", first, second);
}

int main()
{
   char *str;
   char names[4][20] = {
                     "smith/jane",
                     "edwards/john",
                     "stone/dave",
                     "anderson/kenneth",
                  };

   for(int i=0; i<4; i++)
   {
      str = names[i];
      tokenizeString(str);
   }
```

```
        return 0;
}
```

Listing 6.2 starts with the function `tokenizeString()` that invokes the `strtok()` function in order to obtain the first token in the string `str`. This first token is assigned to the string `second` because it's the last name (not the first name). The next portion of `tokenizeString()` contains a loop that repeatedly invokes the `strtok()` function until we read the end of `str`. Notice that each invocation of the `strtok()` function is assigned to the string `first`. Since there are only two names in `str`, it's correct to make this assignment; i.e., the `while` loop will terminate after the first invocation of the `strtok()` function.

However, if `str` contains multiple occurrences of the given delimiter, we would need to replace the `while` loop with the following code block:

```
// print token after delimiter
while (token != NULL)
{
    token = strtok(NULL, delim);
    first = token;
    if(++count == 1) break;
}
```

The `main()` function initializes the array `names` with four names that are in reverse order (e.g., "Smith/John"). The next portion of the `main()` function contains a loop that iterates through the elements of the `names` array and invokes the function `tokenizeString()`. The output is here:

```
NAME: jane smith
NAME: john edwards
NAME: dave stone
NAME: kenneth anderson
```

POINTERS, STRINGS, AND PALINDROMES

A string is a palindrome if the reversed string is the same as the initial string. Listing 6.3 displays the contents of `StringPalindrome.c` that illustrates how to determine whether or not a string is a palindrome.

LISTING 6.3: StringPalindrome.c

```
#include <stdio.h>
#include <string.h>

int scanString(char str[])
{
    int result = 0;
    char *ptr;
    int len = strlen(str);

    for(int i=0; i<len/2; i++)
```

```
   {
      if(str[i] != str[len-i-1])
      {
         result = 1;
         break;
      }
   }

   return result;
}

int main()
{
   int result=0;
   char line1[] = "radar";
   char line2[] = "motion";
   char *results= {"YES", "NO"};

   int len1 = strlen(line1);
   int len2 = strlen(line2);

   result = scanString(line1);
   printf("Current Word: %s\n", line1);
   printf("Palindrome:   %s\n", results[result]);

   result = scanString(line2);
   printf("Current Word: %s\n", line2);
   printf("Palindrome:   %s\n", results[result]);

   return 0;
}
```

Listing 6.3 contains a main() function initializes the pointers ptr1 and str1 with the same hard-coded character string "Hello World" and then defines the character pointer ptr2 that points to location of the variable str1. The rest of the code consists of three printf() statements.

The output from compiling and launching the code in Listing 6.3 is here:

```
Current Word: radar
Palindrome:   YES
Current Word: motion
Palindrome:   NO
```

PASS BY REFERENCE VERSUS VALUE

In Chapter 4, this topic was briefly mentioned, and in this section you will see an example of using a pointer to pass a data structure to a function.

In abstract computer science terms, there is a distinction between "pass by reference" and "pass by value". In a pass by value function call, local copies are made of all the arguments so the function cannot change any data in the calling scope. Pass by reference means that only references to the data are passed, so any changes made by the function affect the actual data in the caller. There is no "pass by reference" mechanism in C, so this behavior is typically emulated by passing a pointer to the actual data. In other languages which have a pass by reference syntax such as C++ or C#, pointers are not used for this purpose.

Listing 6.4 displays the contents of `PassByPointer.c` that illustrates how to pass by reference and by value.

LISTING 6.4: PassByPointer.c

```c
#include <stdio.h>

int  addNumbers1(int a, int b);
void addNumbers2(int a, int b, int *sum);

int addNumbers1(int a, int b)
{
    return (a+b);
}

void addNumbers2(int a, int b, int *sum)
{
    *sum = a+b;
}

int main()
{
    int num1=3, num2=5, sum1, *sum2=&sum1;

    sum1 = addNumbers1(num1, num2);
    printf("%d + %d = %d\n", num1, num2, sum1);

    addNumbers2(2*num1, 3*num2, sum2);
    printf("%d + %d = %d\n", 2*num1, 3*num2, *sum2);

    return 0;
}
```

Listing 6.4 is straightforward: it initializes two integer-valued variables, declaring another integer-valued variable, and then initializes an integer-valued pointer to the location of the third variable.

Next, the function `addNumbers1()` is invoked with `num1` and `num2` and then the function `addNumbers2()` is invoked with `2*num1`, `3*num2`, and `sum2`. After each method invocation the values of various variables are printed.

Notice that the function `addNumbers1()` returns an integer, whereas the function `addNumbers2()` updates the value of the third parameter sum (i.e., it does not return a value). The integer-valued variable `sum2` is highlighted in bold so that you can easily trace the execution sequence and observe the results.

The output from Listing 6.4 is here, with the results that you probably expected:

```
3 + 5 = 8
6 + 15 = 21
```

PASS AN ARRAY BY POINTER

In the context of a function call, an array is treated as if it were a pointer to the first element. This means that it is not possible to pass an array by value, only by reference. Listing 6.5 displays the contents of PassArrayByPointer.c that illustrates how to pass an array of integers by reference.

LISTING 6.5: PassArrayByPointer.c

```c
#include <stdio.h>

void multiplyArray2(int factor, int a[], int *result)
{
    for(int i=0; a[i] != '\0'; i++)
    {
        *(result+i) = factor*a[i];
    }
}

int main()
{
    int arr1[] = {1,2,3,4,5}, factor=3, *result=arr1;

    printf( "Initial Values:\n" );
    for(int i=0; arr1[i] != '\0'; i++)
    {
        printf( "%d ", arr1[i]);
    }
    printf( "\n" );

    multiplyArray2(factor, arr1, result);

    printf( "Updated Values:\n" );
    for(int i=0; arr1[i] != '\0'; i++)
    {
        printf( "%d ", arr1[i]);
    }
    printf( "\n" );

    return 0;
}
```

Listing 6.5 contains the function multiplyArray2() that multiplies the values of an array a (a parameter of the function) by a number, both of which are arguments to the function. The updated contents of the array arr1 are accessible via the third parameter, which is a pointer to an integer-based array. The updated contents of the array are also present in arr1, because the array was not copied but passed by reference.

Next, the main() function initializes an array arr1 with values, assigns the value 3 to the variable factor, and then initializes the pointer-based variable result with the address of arr1.

The `main()` function contains two loops, both of which display the values in the array `arr1`. However, the first loop prints the initial values of the array `arr1`, and the second loop prints the initial values of the array `arr1` after the `multiplyArray2()` function has been invoked. Notice that this function doubles the values of every element of the array `arr1`.

The output from Listing 6.5 is here:

```
Initial Values:
1 2 3 4 5
Updated Values:
3 6 9 12 15
```

A FOR LOOP WITH POINTERS TO NUMBERS

Listing 6.6 displays the contents of `Palindromes1.c` that illustrates how to determine whether a string is a palindrome. In case you have forgotten, a palindrome is a number or string that is a "mirror image" of itself, such as 12321, "rotor," and "radar," whereas 1231 and "rattan" are not palindromes.

LISTING 6.6: Palindromes1.c

```c
#include <stdio.h>
#include <stdio.h>
#include <string.h>

int scanString(char str[])
{
    int result = 0;
    char *ptr;
    int len = strlen(str);

    for(int i=0; i<len/2; i++)
    {
        if(str[i] != str[len-i-1])
        {
            result = 1;
            break;
        }
    }

    return result;
}

int main()
{
    int result=0;
    char line1[] = "radar";
    char line2[] = "motion";
    char *results= {"YES", "NO"};

    int len1 = strlen(line1);
    int len2 = strlen(line2);
```

```
    result = scanString(line1);
    printf("Current Word: %s\n", line1);
    printf("Palindrome:   %s\n", results[result]);

    result = scanString(line2);
    printf("Current Word: %s\n", line2);
    printf("Palindrome:   %s\n", results[result]);

    return 0;
}
```

Listing 6.6 contains the C function scanString with a loop that starts at the value 0 and final value of len /2, which is half the number of elements in the string str. The loop progressively moves in a left-to-right fashion, comparing the contents of the character in the current position with the corresponding character at the "other end" of the string line1.

For example, the number 1234321 compares the left-side digit 1 with the corresponding digit at right-position of this number (which is also a 1). Next, the left-side digit 2 matches the right-side digit 2, followed by comparing the left-side digit 3 with its right-side counterpart. The middle digit does not have a counterpart position, which means that we have verified that the number 1234321 is in fact a palindrome.

Following the same procedure described in the preceding paragraph, the strings "rotor" and "radar" are palindromes, but the number 12345321 is not a palindrome (it's missing a corresponding digit 4).

Compile the code in Listing 6.6 and launch the executable Palindromes1 and you will see the following output:

```
Current Word: radar
Palindrome:   YES
Current Word: motion
Palindrome:   NO
```

POINTERS, LOOPS, AND DIVISORS OF A NUMBER

Listing 6.7 contains a while loop, conditional logic, and the % (modulus) operator in order to find the factors of any integer greater than 1.

LISTING 6.7: Divisors2.c

```
#include <stdio.h>
#include <stdlib.h>
#include <string.h>

int main()
{
    char *primes, prime[20];
    int div=2, num=12;

    printf("Number: %d\n", num);
```

```
while(num > 1)
{
    if(num % div == 0)
    {
        // convert number to string
        sprintf(prime, "%d", div);

        // append string to main string
        asprintf(&primes, "%s %s", primes, prime);

        num /= div;
    }
    else
    {
        ++div;
    }
}

printf("Divisors: %s\n", primes);

return 0;
}
```

The main difference between Listing 6.7 and Listing 6.6 is that the latter constructs the variable divList (which is a concatenated list of the divisors of a number) in the while loop, and then returns the value of divList when the while loop is completed. The output from Listing 6.7 is here:

```
Number: 12
Divisors: (null) 2 2 3
```

Please keep in mind that the asprintf() function was only standardized recently in the Dynamic Memory Technical Report and is not in the C standard proper. This function is only available if __STD_ALLOC_LIB__ is defined by the compiler, and if the user defines __STDC_WANT_LIB_EXT2__ to 1 before including string.h.

POINTERS AND ARRAYS OF NUMBERS

Listing 6.8 displays the contents of PointersArrayNums1.c that illustrates how to initialize strings and pointers.

LISTING 6.8: PointersArrayNums1.c

```
#include <stdio.h>

int main()
{
    int numbers[] = {1,2,3,4,5};
    int *ptr1 = numbers;
    int size1 = sizeof(numbers)/sizeof(int);
```

```
for(int i=0; i<size1; i++)
{
    printf("%d\n", *(ptr1+i));
}

//see what happens when you use these invalid lines:
//for(int ptr1=numbers; ptr1 != NULL; ptr1++)
//for(int *ptr1=&numbers[0]; *ptr1 != '\0'; ptr1++)
//for(int *ptr1=&numbers[0]; *ptr1; ptr1++)

return 0;
}
```

Listing 6.8 is straightforward: the `main()` function initializes the array `numbers` with five integer values, and then initializes the pointer `ptr1` to the location of the numbers array.

The next portion of the `main()` method contains a loop that iterates through the values in the `numbers` array and prints their values. The output from launching the code in Listing 6.8 is here:

```
1
2
3
4
5
```

ARRAY OF POINTERS

Listing 6.9 displays the contents of `ArrayOfPointers.c` that illustrates how to initialize an array of pointers.

LISTING 6.9: ArrayOfPointers.c

```
#include <stdio.h>

int main()
{
    int a=100, b=-200, c=500;
    int *p[3];

    p[0]= &a;
    p[1]= &b;
    p[2]= &c;

    printf("Initial a: %d b: %d c: %d\n",*p[0],*p[1],*p[2]);

    *p[0] += 100;
    *p+= 200;
    *p+= 300;

    printf("Updated a: %d b: %d c: %d\n",*p[0],*p[1],*p[2]);
```

```
        return 0;
}
```

Listing 6.9 initializes three integer-valued variables a, b, and c with the values 100, -200, and 500, respectively. The next code snippet is the declaration of the pointer array p of size 3. The elements p[0], p[1], and pare initialized with the address of the variables a, b, and c, respectively.

Next, the locations p[0], p[1], and p are incremented by the values 100, 200, an 300, respectively, and a printf() statements displays their values. The output from launching the code in Listing 6.9 is here:

```
Initial a: 100 b: -200 c: 500
Updated a: 200 b: 0 c: 800
```

POINTERS AND FUNCTIONS

This section contains an example of passing a pointer-based variable to a function to modify the value of a variable. Note that an example of a pointer to a function (which is different from the concept in this section) is displayed later in this chapter.

Listing 6.10 displays the contents of PointersAndFunctions1.c that illustrates how to initialize strings and pointers.

LISTING 6.10: PointersAndFunctions1.c

```
#include <stdio.h>

void test(int *num)
{
    *num += 6;
    printf("num inside test: %d\n", *num);
}

int main()
{
    int num = 7;

    printf("num before test: %d\n", num);

    test(&num);

    printf("num after  test: %d\n", num);

    return 0;
}
```

Listing 6.10 contains the function test() that increments its pointer-based parameter with 6 and then displays the new value. The main() function initializes the variable num with the value 7, and then displays the value of num before as well as after invoking the function `test()`. The output from launching the code in Listing 6.9 is here:

```
num before test: 7
num inside test: 13
num after  test: 13
```

POINTERS AND ARRAYS OF DECIMALS

Listing 6.11 displays the contents of `PointersDecimals1.c` that illustrates how to initialize strings and pointers.

LISTING 6.11: PointersDecimals1.c

```c
#include <stdio.h>

int main()
{
    int ints1[] = {1.0,2.0,3.0,4.0,5.0};
    int *ptr1  = ints1;
    int isize1 = sizeof(ints1)/sizeof(int);

    int floats1[] = {1.0,2.0,3.0,4.0,5.0};
    int *ptr2  = floats1;
    int fsize1 = sizeof(floats1)/sizeof(float);

    double doubles1[] = {1.0,2.0,3.0,4.0,5.0};
    double *ptr3  = doubles1;
    int dsize1 = sizeof(doubles1)/sizeof(double);

    printf("The ints1 array:\n");
    for(int i=0; i<isize1; i++)
    {
        printf("%d ", *(ptr1+i));
    }
    printf("\n");

    for(int i=0; i<isize1; i++)
    {
        printf("%f ", *(ptr1+i));
    }
    printf("\n");

    printf("The floats1 array:\n");
    for(int i=0; i<fsize1; i++)
    {
        printf("%d ", *(ptr2+i));
    }
    printf("\n");

    for(int i=0; i<fsize1; i++)
    {
        printf("%f ", *(ptr2+i));
    }
    printf("\n");
```

```
printf("The doubles1 array:\n");
for(int i=0; i<dsize1; i++)
{
    printf("%d ", *(ptr2+i));
}
printf("\n");

for(int i=0; i<dsize1; i++)
{
    printf("%f ", *(ptr3+i));
}
printf("\n");

return 0;
}
```

Listing 6.11 contains three arrays ints1, floats1, and doubles1 that contain the same set of decimal values, along with the pointers ptr1, ptr2, and ptr3 that "point" to each of these arrays. The next portion of Listing 6.11 contains three "pairs" of for loops, each of which displays the contents one of the arrays. For instance, the first pair of loops displays the contents of the ints1 array in two ways: the first loop contains a printf() statement with the %d format and the second loop uses a printf() statement with the %f format.

Look closely at the declarations for the three arrays and the way the values in the arrays are printed: are the results consistent with your predictions? The output from launching the code in Listing 6.11 is here:

```
The ints1 array:
1 2 3 4 5
0.000000 0.000000 0.000000 0.000000 0.000000
The floats1 array:
1 2 3 4 5
0.000000 0.000000 0.000000 0.000000 0.000000
The doubles1 array:
1 2 3 4 5
1.000000 2.000000 3.000000 4.000000 5.000000
```

"REVERSING" AN ARRAY OF NUMBERS

The code sample in this section for "reversing" an array of numbers does not work because of an intentional bug (can you find the bug and fix it?). Listing 6.12 displays the contents of ReverseArrayNums1.c that *seems* to reverse an array of numbers using a pointer.

LISTING 6.12: ReverseArrayNums1.c

```
#include <stdio.h>

int main()
{
    // int array with 6 elements
```

```
int arr1[6] = {1,2,3,4,5,6};
int *ptr1, count=6;

printf("Initial:  ");
for(int i=0; i<count; i++)
{
    printf("%d ",arr1[i]);
}
printf("\n");

for(int i=0; i<count/2; i++)
{
    ptr1 = &arr1[i];
printf("ptr = %d ", *ptr1);

    arr1[i] = arr1[count-i-1];
printf("left = %d ", arr1[i]);

    arr1[count-i-1] = *ptr1;
printf("right = %d\n", *ptr1);
}

printf("Reversed: ");
for(int i=0; i<count; i++)
{
    printf("%d ",arr1[i]);
}
printf("\n");

return 0;
}
```

Listing 6.12 contains a main() function that initializes the array arr1 with a set of integers, and then declares the integer pointer ptr1 and the integer count (whose initial value is 6).

The next portion of the main() function contains a loop that iterates through the elements of the array arr1 and displays the values of those elements. The second loop iterates through the first half of the array arr1 and "swaps" each element with its counterpart in the right half of the array arr1.

The logic is very similar to the code that checks for palindromes, with code that uses the pointer ptr1 as a temporary storage location in order to switch the two values.

As you can see in the code, the "counterpart" of the element arr1[i] is arr1[count-i-1]. The final loop iterates through the elements of the array arr1 (which have been reversed). The output from launching the code in Listing 6.12 is here:

```
Initial:  1 2 3 4 5 6
ptr = 1 left = 6 right = 6
ptr = 2 left = 5 right = 5
ptr = 3 left = 4 right = 4
Reversed: 6 5 4 4 5 6
```

The loop in Listing 6.12 attempts to swap by executing this code sequence: a = b; b = a; a = b; which obviously does not perform a swap: it simply assigns b to a. The solution involves performing a *correct* swap. The purpose of this code sample is to show you how easy it is to write buggy C code that looks correct.

MEMORY ALLOCATION FUNCTIONS IN C

The C programming language supports several functions that enable you to dynamically allocate (and free) memory in a C program:

```
malloc()
calloc()
realloc()
free()
```

The malloc() function allocates a block memory in C programs, which is very useful when you define custom structures (as discussed in chapter 6).

The calloc() function allocates a block of memory (just like the malloc() function) and also initializes the allocated memory to zero.

The realloc() function resizes a memory block that was allocated by malloc() or calloc(). If there is sufficient room after the memory block, or if the block is shrinking, it may be possible to do the reallocation in place. If the memory block needs to be reallocated in a new location, the existing data will be copied to the new block and the old block will be freed.

The free() function has the opposite purpose: it frees the memory that was allocated by the functions malloc(), calloc(), realloc(). *Failure to invoke the* free() *function after dynamically allocating memory causes memory leaks.*

Use the malloc() function to copy strings and the strncpy() function to specify the number of characters that you want to copy, or use the strdup() function to allocated memory and copy an entire string in one operation.

The next few sections contain code samples that illustrate how to dynamically allocate memory in C.

THE BUILT-IN MALLOC() C FUNCTION

Listing 6.13 displays the contents of CopyFunction2.c that illustrates how to use the malloc() function and the strncpy() function.

LISTING 6.13: CopyFunction2.c

```c
#include <stdio.h>
#include <stdlib.h>
#include <string.h>

int main()
{
    char *src = "This is one line of text";
```

```
    char *dest;
    int len;
    len = strlen(src);

    dest = (char *)malloc(sizeof(src));

    // fill up 'dest'
    strncpy(dest, src, len);

    // not required because 'strncpy' adds a null
terminator:
    //dest[len-1] = '\0';

    printf("len:   %d\n", len);
    printf("src:   %s\n", src);
    printf("dest: %s\n", dest);
}
```

Listing 6.13 initializes the character pointer src to a hard-coded string, declares the character pointer dest, and sets the value of the integer variable len to the length of the string that is referenced by the variable src.

As you can see in the code section that is shown in bold, the code invokes the built-in C function malloc() to allocate a block of memory whose size is the length of the hard-coded string. In addition, the result is cast as a character pointer and assigned to the character pointer dest.

The next section of code uses the built-in C function strncpy() to copy the contents of the hard-coded string to the memory location that starts at the location "pointed to" by the character pointer dest. The last section contains three printf() statements to display the values of len, src, and dest. The output from launching Listing 6.13 is here:

```
len:   24
src:   This is one line of text
dest: This is one line of text
```

Earlier in the chapter you learned that the malloc() function is "paired" with the free() function in order to deallocate memory that was allocated in a C program. In Listing 6.1 the code prints several values and then immediately terminates normally, so you won't encounter issues due to the absence of a free() invocation. However, if your program is "active" for a period of time and continues to allocate memory without ever freeing that memory, then you will have what is commonly called a "memory leak."

JAGGED ARRAYS

This section contains a C program that illustrates how to work with jagged arrays, which are arrays that contain elements of different lengths. For example, you can define an array of names, where each name is a string of a different length.

Listing 6.14 displays the contents of `JaggedArray1.c` that shows you how to calculate the sum of the entries in a multi-dimensional array.

LISTING 6.14: JaggedArrays.c

```c
#include <stdio.h>
#include <stdlib.h>

int main()
{
    int rowLengths[] = {6,4,3,5};
    int *jagged[4];

    for (int i = 0; i < 4; ++i)
    {
        jagged[i] = (int *)malloc(sizeof(int) *
rowLengths[i]);
    }

    for (int i=0; i<4; ++i)
    {
        for (int j=0; j<rowLengths[i]; ++j)
        {
            jagged[i][j] = i + j + i*j;
            printf("element (%d,%d) = %d\n", i, j, ja[i][j]);
        }
    }
}
```

Listing 6.14 initializes the integer array `rowLengths` with the lengths of 4 rows. Next, the variable `jagged` is declared as a pointer to an array of 4 integer-valued pointers.

The first loop iterates through the 4 rows of `jagged`, and uses the built-in `malloc()` C function to allocate memory for the number of integers that are specified in the `rowLengths` array. For instance, `jagged[0]` is initialized as a pointer to 6 integers, whereas `jagged` is initialized as a pointer to 4 integers.

The second loop is a nested loop that initializes the value of the "cell" at position (i,j) with the value $i + j + i*j$, and then immediately displays that value via the `printf()` function. Launch the code in Listing 6.14 and you will see the following output:

```
element (0,0) = 0
element (0,1) = 1
element (0,2) = 2
element (0,3) = 3
element (0,4) = 4
element (0,5) = 5
element (1,0) = 1
element (1,1) = 3
element (1,2) = 5
element (1,3) = 7
element (2,0) = 2
```

```
element (2,1) = 5
element (2,2) = 8
element (3,0) = 3
element (3,1) = 7
element (3,2) = 11
element (3,3) = 15
element (3,4) = 19
```

USER INPUT, POINTERS, MALLOC (), AND FREE ()

Listing 6.15 displays the contents of PointersToNumbers1.c that illustrates how to print the values (and the addresses) of the elements in a simple character array.

LISTING 6.15: MallocFree.c

```
#include <stlib.h>
#include <stdio.h>

int main()
{
    int size=-1, i;
    int* array;

    do {
        printf("Enter a positive integer: ");
        scanf("%d", &size);
    } while (size <= 0);

    array = (int *)malloc(sizeof(int) * size);

    if (array == NULL) {
        printf("An error creating the dynamic array has
occurred.\n");
        return -1;
    }

    for (i = 0; i < size; i++) {
        array[i] = 1;
        printf("array[%d] has been assigned value 1.\n",
i);
    }

    free(array);

    return 0;
}
```

Listing 6.15 is another straightforward code sample: it starts by initializing a pointer to an integer array called array, followed by a do-while loop that prompts users for a positive integer (and only exits the loop when such a value is entered).

The next portion of the code invokes the built-in C function malloc() in order to allocate a block of memory whose length is equal to the inputted positive integer. After ensuring that the memory allocation was successful, a loop initializes all the element values to 1 in the array called `array`. The last section of code invokes the built-in C function `free()` in order to release the memory that was previously allocated.

An example of the type of output from launching the code in Listing 6.15 is here:

```
Enter a positive integer: -3
Enter a positive integer: 5
array[0] has been assigned value 1.
arrayhas been assigned value 1.
arrayhas been assigned value 1.
arrayhas been assigned value 1.
array[4] has been assigned value 1.
```

Note that if you want to make the code more robust, you need additional code that disallows non-integer decimal values, alphabetic letters, and special characters.

One more point. If the variable `size` is uninitialized, the `do/while` loop has undefined behavior if users enter an invalid input. If we initialize the variable `size` with the value -1 (which is shown in bold in Listing 6.15), this undefined behavior will be removed.

Heap versus Stack

The heap and the stack are available for allocating memory in C programs, and they are handled in slightly different ways.

The memory allocation for all variables in the code samples in previous chapters is on the heap. The operating system performs the memory allocation and you need not worry about freeing that memory. On the other hand, memory that is allocated on the heap via one of the `malloc`-related functions must be explicitly deallocated (otherwise you will have a memory leak).

Function parameters and local variables are allocated memory from the stack; anything that is allocated on the stack is automatically deallocated when the associated function completes its execution.

UPPERCASE AND LOWERCASE STRINGS IN C

The `toupper()` and `tolower()` functions convert letters to uppercase and lowercase, respectively. Listing 6.16 displays the contents of `UpperLowerCase.c` that illustrates how to convert characters to uppercase and lowercase letters.

LISTING 6.16: UpperLowerCase.c

```
#include <stdio.h>
#include <stdlib.h>
#include <string.h>
#include <ctype.h>
```

```
int main()
{
   char *src = "This Is A Line";
   char *lower, *upper, *chr;
   int len;
   len = strlen(src);

   lower = (char *)malloc(sizeof(src));
   strncpy(lower, src, len);
   lower[len-1] = '\0';

   upper = (char *)malloc(sizeof(src));
   strncpy(upper, src, len);

   for(int i=0; i<len; i++)
   {
      *(lower+i) = tolower(src[i]);
      *(upper+i) = toupper(src[i]);
   }

   printf("Original: %s\n", src);
   printf("Upper:    %s\n", upper);
   printf("Lower:    %s\n", lower);
}
```

Listing 6.16 assigns a character string variable src to a hard-coded string, and declares the character pointers lower, upper, and chr.

The character pointers lower and upper are assigned a memory location of a dynamically allocated block of memory via the malloc() method, after which the hard-coded character string is copied (via the strncpy() function) into the location of the variables lower and upper. As you saw in an earlier example, the strncpy() function automatically null terminates both pointers.

The next section of code is a loop that iterates from 0 to len and covers the characters in the lower pointer and upper pointer to lowercase and uppercase, via the built-in C functions tolower() and toupper(), respectively. The last portion of code displays the strings pointed to by src, lower, and upper.

One other detail: many of the code samples in this chapter use the syntax *(lower+i), but you can also use the more idiomatic syntax lower[i]. The output from Listing 6.16 is here:

```
Original: This Is A Line
Upper:    THIS IS A LINE
Lower:    this is a line
```

REVERSING A STRING

Earlier in the chapter you saw an example of reversing the integer elements of an array, and this section shows you how to reverse a string. Listing 6.17 displays the contents of ReverseString1.c that illustrates how to reverse a hard-coded string in a dynamically allocated block of memory.

LISTING 6.17: ReverseString1.c

```c
#include <stdio.h>
#include <stdlib.h>
#include <string.h>

int main()
{
   char *ptr1 = "this is a string";
   char *ptr2;
   int len=strlen(ptr1);

   ptr2 = (char *)malloc(len);

   for(int i=0; i<len; i++)
   {
      *(ptr2+len-1-i) = *(ptr1+i);
   }

   printf("Original: %s\n", ptr1);
   printf("Reverse:  %s\n", ptr2);
}
```

Listing 6.17 contains a `main()` function that initializes the character pointer `ptr1` to a hard-coded string, and declares the character pointer `ptr2`. The length of the character string at `ptr1` is assigned to the integer variable `len`, and `ptr2` is assigned the address of a block of memory that is as long as the string at location `ptr1`.

The next section of code is a loop that iterates through the characters of the string at the location of `ptr1`. During each left-to-right iteration through the string `ptr1`, the positions at the "far end" of `ptr2` are assigned the characters from left-to-right iteration through the characters in `ptr1`. If you read the code carefully you can see that the characters at `ptr2` are the reverse order of the characters at `ptr1`. The output from Listing 6.17 is here:

```
Original: this is a string
Reverse:  gnirts a si siht
```

FINDING UPPERCASE AND LOWERCASE LETTERS

Listing 6.18 displays the contents of `UpperAndLowerCount.c` that illustrates how to construct strings with only uppercase and only lowercase letters from a text string. This code has a subtle bug (can you find it?) that is explained in the discussion after the code listing.

LISTING 6.18: UpperAndLowerCount.c

```c
#include <stdio.h>
#include <stdlib.h>
#include <string.h>
#include <ctype.h>
```

```
int main()
{
    char str1[] = "This is a String";
    char *lower1, *upper1;
    int lcount=0, ucount=0;

    int len1 = strlen(str1);
    lower1 = (char *)malloc(len1);
    upper1 = (char *)malloc(len1);

    for(int i=0; i<len1; i++)
    {
        if(str1[i] == tolower(str1[i]))
        {
            *(lower1+lcount) = str1[i];
            lcount++;
        }
        else if(str1[i] == toupper(str1[i]))
        {
            *(upper1+ucount) = str1[i];
            ucount++;
        }

/*
        // correct code:
        if(islower(str1[i]))
        {
            *(lower1+lcount) = str1[i];
            lcount++;
        }
        else if(isupper(str1[i]))
        {
            *(upper1+ucount) = str1[i];
            ucount++;
        }
*/

    }

    *(lower1+lcount) = '\0';
    *(upper1+ucount) = '\0';

    printf("Original:  %s\n",str1);
    printf("Lowercase: %s\n",lower1);
    printf("Uppercase: %s\n",upper1);

    return 0;
}
```

Listing 6.18 is similar to the earlier code samples that use the built-in C function `malloc()`, which in this case dynamically allocates memory for the character pointers `lower1` and `upper1`. A loop iterates through the letters in the character array `str1` and uses conditional logic to check if the current letter is lowercase or uppercase (the third case is any other printable character, which is ignored in this code sample). In the former case, the current character is "appended" to the list of lowercase letters; in the latter case, the current character is "appended" to the list of uppercase letters.

After null-terminating the newly constructed strings, three `printf()` statements display the value of `str1`, `lower1`, and `upper1`. The output from launching `UpperAndLower` is here:

```
Original:  This is a String
Lowercase: his is a tring
Uppercase: TS
```

The conditional logic in Listing 6.18 appears correct: however, this logic treats spaces and punctuation as lowercase or uppercase, neither of which will change when they are passed to the `tolower()` or to the `toupper()` functions. Fortunately, the solution is simple: use `if(islower(str1[i]))` and `if(isupper(str1[i]))` to determine whether a letter is lowercase or uppercase, respectively. This solution is also clearer than the incorrect code.

REMOVING WHITESPACES FROM A STRING

Listing 6.19 displays the contents of `RemoveWhiteSpaces.c` that illustrates how to remove whitespaces from a string.

LISTING 6.19: RemoveWhiteSpaces.c

```c
#include <stdio.h>
#include <stdlib.h>
#include <string.h>
#include <ctype.h>

int main()
{
    char str1[] = "This is a String";
    char *ptr1;
    int count=0;

    int len1 = strlen(str1);
    ptr1= (char *)malloc(len1);

    for(int i=0; i<len1; i++)
    {
        if((str1[i] == ' ') || (str1[i] == '\t'))
        {
            continue;
        }
        else
        {
            *(ptr1+count) = str1[i];
            count++;
        }
    }

    *(ptr1+count) = '\0';
```

```
printf("Original:   %s\n",str1);
printf("Stripped:   %s\n",ptr1);

return 0;
}
```

Listing 6.19 starts by initializing the character array `str1` and declaring the character pointer `ptr1`. Next, a loop iterates through the characters in the character array `str1`, and if any character is not whitespace (either blank or a tab character), then that character is "appended" to the list of characters that are not whitespaces.

Notice that the variable `i` is the index variable in the loop, whereas the variable `count` keeps track of the number of characters that are not whitespaces, and equals the number of such characters at any point during the loop iteration. The output from compiling and launching the code in Listing 6.19 is here:

```
Original:   This is a String
Stripped:   ThisisaString
```

POINTERS, STRINGS, AND CHARACTER COUNTS

C does not provide support for structures such as hash tables, which means that you have to provide your own implementation or use a third party implementation (which is preferable if it is mature and stable).

A compromise of sorts is to create an array to keep track of the distinct characters in a given string, and another array to keep track of the number of times that each character appears in that string. The first array would have length 52 if you are keeping track of uppercase and lowercase letters, and if you want to accommodate punctuation and special characters, you would need an array of size 100 (approximately). Keep in mind that this number will increase for some other languages, and it's impractical for writing systems such as Kanji.

Notice that the preceding scenario does not comprise a hash table: a hash table has "lookup time" $O(1)$ for any character, whereas the lookup time for an array is $O(n)$, where n is the number of elements in the array. Note that the "lookup time" in the previous sentence refers to the time required to find an element in an unsorted array. If you perform a linear search in an array, the expected number of searches required to find an element is $n/2$, and the latter is $O(n)$.

However, if you store the unique characters of larger documents (100K and above) in an array, and you also store their frequencies in another array, then the lookup time is no greater than the number of characters that exist for the language in which the document is written.

Listing 6.20 displays the contents of `CharCounts.c` that illustrates how to initialize strings and pointers.

LISTING 6.20: CharCounts.c

```c
#include <stdio.h>
#include <stdio.h>
#include <stdlib.h>
#include <string.h>

int main()
{
    char ch, str1[] = "This is a string with some short
words that wraps around and let's see how well the code in
this code sample actually works!";

    int len1 = strlen(str1);

    // incorrect:
    // int *chars = malloc (sizeof (char) * len1);
    // correct:
    char *chars = malloc (sizeof (char) * len1);

    int *counts = malloc (sizeof (int) * len1);
    int i;

    for (i=0; i<len1; i++)
    {
      counts[i] = 0;
      chars[i]  = ' ';
    }

    int pos=0, foundchar=0;
    counts[pos] = 1;
    chars[pos]  = str1[0];
    pos = 1;

    for(int i=1; i<len1; i++)
    {
        ch = str1[i];
 //printf("checking char %c at pos: %d\n",ch, i);

        foundchar = 0;
        for(int k=0; k<pos; k++)
        {
            if(ch == chars[k])
            {
                ++counts[k];
 //printf("count for %c at pos %d : %d\n",ch, k,
counts[k]);
                foundchar = 1;
                break;
            }
        }

        if(foundchar == 0)
        {
 //printf("inserting char %c at pos: %d\n",ch, pos);
            counts[pos] = 1;
```

```
        chars[pos]   = ch;
        ++pos;
    }
}

printf("Full string: %s\n",str1);

char ch2;
int count;
for(int k=0; k<pos; k++)
{
    printf("char %c count %d at array position: %d\n",
        chars[k], counts[k], k);
}

return 0;
}
```

Listing 6.20 has a main() function that initializes the character string str1 and then uses the built-in C function malloc() to dynamically allocate memory for the character pointer chars and the integer pointer counts.

A simple loop then initializes all the entries of chars with a blank space (' ') and all the entries of counts with 0. The middle portion of the code contains a large for loop that counts the number of unique characters in the original string str1. During each loop iteration, an inner loop checks if the current character has already detected; if so, the position of that character in the counts array is incremented. If not, then the current character is appended to the chars array and its corresponding value in the counts array is set to 1.

The final block of code in Listing 6.20 iterates through the chars array and prints each element, along with its count (which is stored in the counts array). The output from compiling and launching the code in Listing 6.20 is here:

Full string: This is a string with some short words that wraps around and let's see how well the code in this code sample actually works!

```
char T count 1 at array position: 0
char h count 7 at array position: 1
char i count 6 at array position: 2
char s count 12 at array position: 3
char   count 23 at array position: 4
char a count 8 at array position: 5
char t count 9 at array position: 6
char r count 6 at array position: 7
char n count 4 at array position: 8
char g count 1 at array position: 9
char w count 6 at array position: 10
char o count 8 at array position: 11
char m count 2 at array position: 12
char e count 9 at array position: 13
char d count 5 at array position: 14
char p count 2 at array position: 15
char u count 2 at array position: 16
```

```
char l count 6 at array position: 17
char ' count 1 at array position: 18
char c count 3 at array position: 19
char y count 1 at array position: 20
char k count 1 at array position: 21
char ! count 1 at array position: 22
```

POINTERS TO FUNCTIONS OF TYPE VOID

Listing 6.21 displays the contents of PointersNums1.c that illustrates how to define two simple functions and also a function pointer in order to "point" to those functions and execute them.

LISTING 6.21: PointersToVoidFunctions1.c

```c
#include <stdio.h>

void one()
{
    printf("Inside function one\n");
}

void two()
{
    printf("Inside function two\n");
}

int main()
{
    void (*ptr1)();

    one();
    ptr1 = &one;
    (*ptr1)();
    //ptr1 = one;
    //ptr1();


    two();
    ptr1 = &two;
    (*ptr1)();
}
```

Listing 6.21 starts with the definition of the functions one() and two(), both of which have return type void. They contain a single printf() statement that identifies the current function that has been executed.

The next portion of Listing 6.21 contains a main() function that declares a function pointer ptr1 whose return type is void. Next, the function one() is executed, after which ptr1 is initialized to the address of the function one(), and the code snippet (*ptr1)() is executed (which means that the function one() is executed again).

The preceding code block that refers to ptr1 is followed by a commented out code snippet that uses a simpler syntax. On the assignment statement, the

& is unnecessary because bare function names used in a function pointer context decay to a function pointer without any additional syntax, so the syntax ptr1 = one; is a simpler alternate syntax. Also, the function call operation does not require a dereference, so you can invoke ptr1() without any additional syntax.

So, if there are two acceptable syntaxes, why not use the simpler one and ignore the more complicated syntax? The answer is simple: use the simpler syntax, but keep in mind that you will encounter the other syntax in other people's code, so it's important to understand both types of syntax.

The next code block performs the same sort of thing, this type by "pointing" to the function two() instead of the function one(). The output from launching the code in Listing 6.21 is here, and as you can see, the message in function one() is printed twice and then the message inside two() is printed twice:

```
Inside function one
Inside function one
Inside function two
Inside function two
```

POINTERS TO NON-VOID FUNCTIONS

The previous section showed you how to invoke function pointers to functions that have a return type of void. Listing 6.22 displays the contents of the custom function PointersToNonVoidFunctions.c that illustrates how to invoke function pointers to functions that have a non- void return type.

LISTING 6.22: PointersToNonVoidFunctions1.c

```c
#include <stdio.h>

int add(int x, int y)
{
    printf("Inside add\n");
    return (x+y);
}

int multiply(int x, int y, int z)
{
    printf("Inside multiply\n");
    return (x*y*z);
}

int main()
{
    int result, x=3, y=4, z=5;

    int (*ptr1)(int, int);
    int (*ptr2)(int, int, int);

    result = add(x,y);
    printf("Result1:  %d\n", result);
```

```
        ptr1 = &add;
        result = (*ptr1)(x,y);
        printf("Result2:   %d\n", result);
        printf("-------------\n");

        result = multiply(x,y,z);
        printf("Result3:   %d\n", result);

        ptr2 = &multiply;
        result = (*ptr2)(x,y,z);
        printf("Result4:   %d\n", result);
}
```

Listing 6.22 starts with the definition of the function add() that returns the sum of two integers, followed by the definition of the function multiply() that returns the product of three integers.

The next portion of Listing 6.22 contains a main() function that contains two prototypes for function pointers ptr1 and ptr2, as shown here:

```
int (*ptr1)(int, int);
int (*ptr2)(int, int, int);
```

Next, the integer-valued variable result is initialized with the value that is returned by executing the function add(), and then the result is displayed. Now the function pointer ptr1 is initialized with the address of the function add(), and when ptr1 is executed (with the same arguments), the result is the same as the preceding output.

The next block of code is similar to the previous section, but with result and ptr2 "pointing" to the function multiply(). The output from launching the code in Listing 6.22 is here:

```
Inside add
Result1:   7
Inside add
Result2:   7
-------------
Inside multiply
Result3:   60
Inside multiply
Result4:   60
```

FUNCTION POINTERS AS ARGUMENTS

Another use for function pointers is to specify function pointers as arguments to a function. Listing 6.23 displays the contents of FunctionPointersAsArgs.c that illustrates how to define a pointer to a function as an argument of another function.

LISTING 6.23: FunctionPointersAsArgs.c
```
#include <stdio.h>
```

```
void squaredValues(int startValue, int endValue, int (*fp)
(int))
{
    printf("Calculating Squared Values\n");
    printf("-------------------------\n");
    for(int x=startValue; x<endValue; x++)
    {
        printf("%2d    %3d\n", x, (*fp)(x));
    }
    printf("\n");
}

int square(int x) {
    return x*x;
}

void cubedValues(int startValue, int endValue, int (*fp)
(int))
{
    printf("Calculating Cubed Values\n");
    printf("-----------------------\n");
    for(int x=startValue; x<endValue; x++)
    {
        printf("%2d    %3d\n", x, (*fp)(x));
    }
}

int cube(int x) {
    return x*x*x;
}

int main()
{
    squaredValues(1, 10, square);
    cubedValues(1, 10, cube);

    return 0;
}
```

Listing 6.23 starts with the definition of the functions squaredValues() and cubedValues(), both of which have return type void, two integer-valued parameters, and a third parameter that is a function pointer whose return type is void. In addition, the functions squared() and cubed() are defined, both of which have return type int.

The next portion of Listing 6.23 contains a main() function where the first line of code invokes the function squaredValues(), as shown here:

```
squaredValues(1, 10, square);
```

The next portion of Listing 6.23 invokes the function cubedValues(), as shown here:

```
cubedValues(1, 10, cube);
```

As you can see, the previous two code snippets specify the functions `square()` and `cube()`, respectively, as their third argument. Contrast this code with previous code samples that passed a function pointer instead of the actual function name. The output from launching the code in Listing 6.23 is here:

```
Calculating Squared Values
--------------------------
1      1
2      4
3      9
4      16
5      25
6      36
7      49
8      64
9      81

Calculating Cubed Values
------------------------
1      1
2      8
3      27
4      64
5      125
6      216
7      343
8      512
9      729
```

If you would rather avoid function pointers, define an array of functions as a function lookup table, or 2) use case statements inside a switch statement.

POINTERS TO POINTERS

In Chapter 5, you learned that it's possible to define a pointer to a pointer in a C program, and now we're going to look at such an example. Listing 6.24 displays the contents of `PointersToPointers.c` that illustrates how to work with pointers to pointers.

LISTING 6.24: PointersToPointers.c

```c
#include <stdio.h>

int main()
{
    char *list[] = {"a", "b", "c", "d", NULL};

    for (char **ptr=list; *ptr != NULL; ptr++){
        printf("array item: %s\n", ptr[0]);
    }

    return 0;
}
```

Listing 6.24 defines a character pointer list that is initialized with the first four letters of the alphabet. Next, a loop iterates through the elements of the character pointer `list`, using the character pointer `ptr`, with the "double asterisk" syntax, which indicates the pointer to the pointer of an address. The output from launching the code in Listing 6.24 is here:

```
array item: a
array item: b
array item: c
array item: d
```

SUMMARY

This chapter introduced more examples of a pointer in C, along with examples of pointers to numbers, arrays, and strings. You saw how to use pointers to split a string, check for palindromes, as well as for loops that use pointers to find the divisors of a number. Next, you learned how to define pointers to arrays of numbers.

Then you saw how to use pointers to reverse a string, how to find uppercase and lowercase letters, and how to remove whitespaces from a string. Then you saw how to count words in a line of text, how to define pointers to functions, and function pointers as arguments. Finally, you learned how to define pointers to pointers and how to process command line arguments.

## CHAPTER 7

MISCELLANEOUS TOPICS

This chapter contains a mix of topics, some of which are more complex than the topics covered in the previous chapters. If you are an absolute beginner, then it might be better for you to postpone a deep study of the topics in this chapter (at least for now). However, it's worthwhile to perform a cursory overview of its contents in case there are code samples with features of C that are relevant for your needs. Either way, most of the topics in this chapter are discussed in a high-level fashion; if you become a full-time C developer you will probably become much more familiar with these topics.

The first part of this chapter discusses the C preprocessor #define, how to define C macros, and bit-level operations in C. If you plan to continue learning about C, these topics are useful and you will encounter them in many C programs.

The second part of this chapter discusses C structs and how to create custom structures that hold various types of data value. You'll also see code samples that show you how to define pointers to C structs, nested C structs, and arrays of C structs. The third part of this chapter covers C features such as C unions, unions combined with structs, and bitfields in C.

The fourth section provides some rudimentary information about system calls in C, along with two related code samples. The final section discusses header files, and how to define and reference local header files in a C program.

SYMBOLIC CONSTANTS

Unlike languages such as Java, C supports a #define keywords that enables you to define a symbolic name or symbolic constant, which is often a number or a string, and its format is shown here:

```
#define   MYNAME   some_text_goes_here
```

For example, the following snippet assigns a number to the string PI:

```
#define PI 3.1415962
```

The C preprocessor (which is external to the C language) uses text substitution in order to replace every occurrence of the string PI in your C program with the value that is defined in the preceding code snippet.

One convenient use of #define is for constants that represent escape sequences. For example, it's convenient to use the following definitions for a linefeed, carriage return, and form feed, whose octal values are 012, 015, and 014, respectively:

```
#define LF '\012'
#define CR '\015'
#define FF '\014'
```

Alternatively, the following definitions specify the hexadecimal values for a linefeed, carriage return, and form feed, respectively:

```
#define LF '\x0A'
#define CR '\x0D'
#define FF '\x0B'
```

As a general rule: use #define statements whenever they improve the clarity of your C programs.

WORKING WITH MACROS IN C

Earlier in this chapter you learned how to use the #define keyword in order to define constants or strings. You can also use the #define keyword to define so-called macros, which comprise a block of executable C code. The C preprocessor uses text substitution to replace the occurrence of each macro with its corresponding definition.

Listing 7.1 displays the contents of SimpleMacro.c that illustrates how to define a macro in C.

LISTING 7.1: SimpleMacro.c

```
#include <stdio.h>

#define add2(num1, num2) { \
    int total=0;           \
    sum = num1 + num2;     \
}

int main()
{
    int sum, num1=5, num2=8;
    add2(num1, num2);
    printf("num1 = %i num2 = %i sum = %i\n", num1, num2,
                                              sum);
```

```
    return 0;
}
```

Listing 7.1 starts with the definition of the macros `add2` that adds two numbers and sets the variable `sum` equal to that value. Notice that the type of `num1` and `num2` are not specified (which differs from functions that have parameters).

The `main()` function declares `sum`, `num1` (initial value is 5), and `num2` (initial value is 8), and then invokes the `add2` macro. Notice that the `add2` macro does not return the value of `sum` (which is 15 in this case). The value of `sum` is assigned in `add2`, the value of `sum` in the `main()` function is updated with the correct value. This functionality is vaguely reminiscent of pass-by-reference, except that the variable `sum` is not passed to the `add2` macro. The output from launching the C program in Listing 7.1 is here:

```
num1 = 5 num2 = 8 sum = 13
```

OTHER OPERATORS IN C

C supports various operators beyond those that you learned in previous chapters, which include: bitwise, logic, shift, and comma operators.

The bitwise operators in C are important for tasks that require working with individual bits in non-trivial ways. Examples include reading from serial and parallel ports and writing data to those ports.

The following subsections provide a brief introduction to bitwise, logical, and comma operators, along with simple code samples.

Bitwise Operators

The bitwise operators in C are `&`, `|`, `^`, `~`, `<<`, and `>>` that correspond to binary AND, binary OR, binary XOR (eXclusive OR), binary Ones complement, binary Left Shift, and binary Right Shift, respectively.

The following example illustrates how to calculate a logical AND of two binary numbers:

```
  11001000
& 10111000
  --------
= 10001000
```

The following example illustrates how to calculate a logical OR of two binary numbers:

```
  11001000
| 00001111
  --------
= 11001111
```

If you need to use any of the other bitwise operators, perform an online search for code samples that contain those operators.

Logical Operators

The logical operators in C are `&&` and `||` that represent logical AND and logical OR, respectively. You already saw one example of logical operators in C: the code sample in Chapter 2 that involves compound conditional logic.

Comma Operator

The comma operator combines the two expressions and evaluates them in a left-to-right order. The value of the right-hand side is returned as the value of the whole expression. An example of the comma operator is here:

```
for (low=0, high=MAXSIZE; low < high; low=newlow,
high=newhigh)
{
    // do something with low and high
}
```

Cumulative Code Sample

Listing 7.2 displays the contents of `BitOperations.c` that illustrates how to compute various bit operations on binary numbers.

LISTING 7.2: BitOperations.c

```
#include <stdio.h>

int main()
{
    // binary literals are a non-standard extension
    int x1 = 0b11001000;
    int x2 = 0b10111000;
    int x3, x4, x5, x6;

    x3 = x1 & x2;
    x4 = x1 | x2;
    x5 = x1 ^ x2;
    x6 = (x1 << 2);

    printf("x1 = %x %d %o\n", x1, x1, x1);
    printf("x2 = %x %d %o\n", x2, x2, x2);
    printf("x3 = %x %d %o\n", x3, x3, x3);
    printf("x4 = %x %d %d\n", x4, x4, x4);
    printf("x5 = %x %d %o\n", x5, x5, x5);
    printf("x6 = %x %d %o\n", x6, x6, x6);

    return 0;
}
```

Listing 7.2 contains a `main()` function that declares the integer variables `x3`, `x4`, `x5`, and `x6`. The next section of code uses the operators `&`, `|`, `^`, and `<<` (discussed earlier) to initialize values for `x3`, `x4`, `x5`, and `x6`. The final block of code consists of six `printf()` statements the display the values of the variables x1 through x6 in hexadecimal, decimal, and octal format. The output from Listing 7.2 is here:

```
x1 = c8 200 310
x2 = b8 184 270
x3 = 88 136 210
x4 = f8 248 248
x5 = 70 112 160
x6 = 320 800 1440
```

Unfortunately, C does not provide a mechanism for displaying binary numbers in the printf() command. However, Listing 7.3 displays the contents of ShowBits.c (borrowed from Wikipedia) that illustrates how to display the digits of a binary number.

LISTING 7.3: ShowBits.c

```c
#include <stdio.h>

void showbits(unsigned int x)
{
    int i;

    for(i=(sizeof(int)*8)-1; i>=0; i--)
    {
        (x&(1u<<i)) ? putchar('1'): putchar('0');
    }

    printf("\n");
}

int main()
{
    int j = 5225, m, n;
    printf("%d in binary \t\t ", j);
    showbits(j);

    // the loop for right shift operation
    for ( m = 0; m <= 5; m++ )
    {
        n = j >> m;
        printf("%d right shift %d gives ", j, m);
        showbits(n);
    }

    return 0;
}
```

Listing 7.3 starts with the function showbits() with a loop that performs a logical left-shift of the unsigned integer 1. During each shift operation, the value of x is "anded" with the current left-shift value: if the result is non-zero then the integer 1 is displayed, otherwise the digit 0 is displayed.

The `main()` function of Listing 7.3 starts by invoking the `showbits()` function with the variable `j` whose value is initially 5225. The next portion of the `main()` function is a for loop that invokes the `showbits()` function with the variable `n` that undergoes a logical right-shift of the variable `j`. This loop executes six times, and displays the output after each invocation of the `showbits()` function. The output from Listing 7.3 is here:

```
5225 in binary          00000000000000000001010001101001
5225 right shift 0 gives 00000000000000000001010001101001
5225 right shift 1 gives 00000000000000000000101000110100
5225 right shift 2 gives 00000000000000000000010100011010
5225 right shift 3 gives 00000000000000000000001010001101
5225 right shift 4 gives 00000000000000000000000101000110
5225 right shift 5 gives 00000000000000000000000010100011
```

THE BUBBLE SORT ALGORITHM

The bubble sort is a well-known algorithm for sorting an array of numbers. This algorithm has $O(n^2)$ complexity, where n is the number of items in the array. Although this book is not about algorithms in C, this section contains the C code for the bubble sort to familiarize you with the C syntax for such an algorithm.

Listing 7.4 displays the contents of `BubbleSort.c` that illustrates how to use the bubble sort in order to sort an array of integers.

LISTING 7.4: BubbleSort.c

```c
#include <stdio.h>

int main()
{
    int numbers[] = {5, 1, 2, 4, 3};
    int count = sizeof(numbers)/sizeof(numbers[0]);
    int temp;

    printf("Original: ");
    for(int i=0; i<count; i++)
    {
        printf("%d ",numbers[i]);
    }
    printf("\n");

    for(int i=0; i<count-1; i++)
    {
        for(int j=i; j<count; j++)
        {
            if(numbers[i] > numbers[j])
            {
                temp = numbers[i];
                numbers[i] = numbers[j];
                numbers[j] = temp;
            }
```

```
    }
  }

  printf("Sorted:    ");
  for(int i=0; i<count; i++)
  {
      printf("%d ",numbers[i]);
  }
  printf("\n");

  return 0;
}
```

Listing 7.4 is a "classical" sorting algorithm, and the code constructs have been covered in previous chapters. After defining an array of integers, the `main()` function contains a nested loop, where the inner loop has conditional logic to determine when to swap two elements of the array. The result of this conditional logic is to "bubble up" the larger elements: i.e., the sorted array starts with the smallest number and ends with the largest number. The output from launching 7.4 is here:

```
Original: 5 1 2 4 3
Sorted:   1 2 3 4 5
```

WHAT IS A C STRUCT?

A C `struct` is essentially a "structure" that defines a group of logically related items. Simple examples of logically related items that can be defined via a C `struct` include: employee, student, mailing address, and so forth. Keep in mind that the data values might be accessed from a file, a database, or retrieved via a Web service.

In addition, you can perform the following operations with C `structs` in your C programs:

- Create arrays of C `structs`
- Copy or assign C `structs`
- Use the & operator with C `structs`
- Pass C `structs` to functions
- Return C `structs` from functions

As you will see in subsequent sections, you can even define a C `struct` inside another C `struct` (such as a customer with a mailing address and a shipping address as separate C `structs`), as well as an array of C `structs` (each of which could represent an employee in the form of a C `struct`).

However, keep in mind that you *cannot* compare two C `structs`: you must perform an element-by-element comparison of two C `structs` via custom code.

The next section shows you an example of creating a simple C struct that contains employee-related information.

An Example of a C struct

Listing 7.5 displays the contents of EmployeeStruct1.c that illustrates how to create a basic structure for employee-related data. A complete C struct for an employee would contain many other fields that you can add to the C struct in this code sample.

LISTING 7.5: EmployeeStruct1.c

```c
#include <stdio.h>
#include <string.h>

typedef struct Employee
{
    char  fname [50];
    char  lname [50];
    char  title [100];
    int   emp_id;
} emp;

int main()
{
    struct Employee emp1;

    strcpy( emp1.fname, "John");
    strcpy( emp1.lname, "Smith");
    strcpy( emp1.title, "Developer");
    emp1.emp_id = 2000;

    printf("First name:   %s\n",emp1.fname);
    printf("Last name:    %s\n",emp1.lname);
    printf("Title:        %s\n",emp1.title);
    printf("Employee id: %d\n",emp1.emp_id);
}
```

Listing 7.5 is very straightforward, starting with the definition of the custom C struct called Employee that contains fields for the first name, last name, title, and employee ID for each employee. As you probably expect, the first three fields are character strings and the fourth field has an integer value (but this field could also be a character string).

The next portion of the main() function uses the built-in C function strcpy() to assign values to the first three character-based fields, and then a simple assignment statement to initialize the integer-valued emp_id field.

The last portion of the main() function contains printf() statements to display the values of the fields in the Employee struct.

Compile the code in Listing 7.5 and launch the executable and you will see the following output:

```
First name:   John
Last name:    Smith
Title:        Developer
Employee id: 2000
```

A POINTER TO A C STRUCT

This section assumes that you have read the relevant pointer-related sections in Chapter 5, and please read that material if you have not already done so.

Listing 7.6 displays the contents of `PointerStructs.c` that illustrates how to create a structure for employee-related data as well as a pointer to such a structure (the new code is shown in bold).

LISTING 7.6: EmployeeStructs.c

```c
#include <stdio.h>
#include <string.h>

typedef struct Employee
{
   char   fname [50];
   char   lname [50];
   char   title [100];
   int    emp_id;
} emp;

int main()
{
   struct Employee emp1;

   strcpy( emp1.fname,  "John");
   strcpy( emp1.lname,  "Smith");
   strcpy( emp1.title,  "Developer");
   emp1.emp_id = 2000;

   printf("First name:   %s\n",emp1.fname);
   printf("Last name:    %s\n",emp1.lname);
   printf("Title:        %s\n",emp1.title);
   printf("Employee id: %d\n",emp1.emp_id);

   struct Employee *empptr = &emp1;
   printf("\nPointer of Employee:\n");
   printf("First name:   %s\n",empptr->fname);
   printf("Last name:    %s\n",empptr->lname);
   printf("Title:        %s\n",empptr->title);
   printf("Employee id: %d\n",empptr->emp_id);
}
```

Listing 7.6 starts with the same definition of `Employee struct` that you saw in Listing 7.5, and also the first two sections of the `main()` function. The third section contains all the new code, which initializes the variable `empptr`. As you can see, `empptr` is a pointer of type `Employee`, and it's initialized with the address of the previously initialized variable emp1 (which is also a C struct of type Employee). Next, a set of printf() statements display the contents of the Employee structure using the "arrow syntax" for the variable empptr.

Compile the code in Listing 7.6 and launch the executable and you will see the following output:

```
First name:  John
Last name:   Smith
Title:       Developer
Employee id: 2000

Pointer of Employee:
First name:  John
Last name:   Smith
Title:       Developer
Employee id: 2000
```

NESTED C STRUCTS

Listing 7.7 displays the contents of NestedStructures.c that illustrates how to define a C struct for employee-related data that contains another C struct.

LISTING 7.7: NestedStructures.c

```c
#include <stdio.h>
#include <string.h>

struct Address
{
    char street[50];
    char city[50];
};

struct Employee
{
    int id;
    char name[20];
    char title[20];
    struct Address address;
} emp;

int main()
{
    struct Employee emp =
        {1000, "John Smith", "Developer", "123 Main Street",
"Chicago"};

    printf("Emp Id: %d \n",   emp.id);
    printf("Name:   %s \n",   emp.name);
    printf("Title:  %s \n\n", emp.title);
```

```c
    printf("Street: %s\n", emp.address.street);
    printf("City:   %s\n", emp.address.city);

    return 0;
}
```

Listing 7.7 starts by defining a custom Address that is a C struct (with two character fields), followed by a user-defined Employee C struct that is similar to previous examples. This time the Employee C struct contains an address element that is of type Address.

Next, the code in the main() function initializes the emp variable with values for the five fields that match the definition of the Employee element. The five elements in the emp element are displayed using printf() statements.

One detail in particular to notice is that the fourth and fifth elements are accessed via emp.address.street and emp.address.city because they match the corresponding strings in the initialization of the variable emp.

Compile the code in Listing 7.7 and launch the executable and you will see the following output:

```
Emp Id: 1000
Name:   John Smith
Title:  Developer

Street: 123 Main Street
City:   Chicago
```

The next section shows you how to create an array of user-defined C struct elements, where each element contains information about an employee.

AN ARRAY OF C STRUCTS

Listing 7.8 displays the contents of ArrayOfEmployees.c that illustrates how to populate an array with C structs.

LISTING 7.8: ArrayOfEmployees.c

```c
#include <stdio.h>
#include <stdlib.h>
#include <string.h>

typedef struct Employee
{
    char   fname [50];
    char   lname [50];
    char   title [100];
    int    emp_id;
} emp;

int main()
{
    int empCount = 5;
```

```c
struct Employee emps[empCount];
struct Employee *empPtr;

char *fnames= {"John", "Jane", "Steve"};
char *lnames[4] = {"Smith", "Jones",
                   "Edwards", "Anderson"};
char *titles[4] = {"Sales", "Marketing",
                   "Development", "Support"};

// initialize array of Employees
for(int i=0; i<empCount; i++)
{
    strcpy(emps[i].fname, fnames[i%3]);
    strcpy(emps[i].lname, lnames[i%4]);
    strcpy(emps[i].title, titles[i%4]);
    emps[i].emp_id = 1000*(i+1);
}

// print contents of all Employees
for(int i=0; i<empCount; i++)
{
    printf("First name:   %s\n",emps[i].fname);
    printf("Last name:    %s\n",emps[i].lname);
    printf("Title:        %s\n",emps[i].title);
    printf("Employee id: %d\n",emps[i].emp_id);
    printf("\n");
}

// print contents of all Employees
for(int i=0; i<empCount; i++)
{
    empPtr = &emps[i];

    printf("First name:   %s\n",empPtr->fname);
    printf("Last name:    %s\n",empPtr->lname);
    printf("Title:        %s\n",empPtr->title);
    printf("Employee id: %d\n",empPtr->emp_id);
    printf("\n");
}

}
```

Listing 7.8 starts with the definition of the (by now familiar) Employee C struct, followed by a lengthy main() function that is not as complicated as you might think. The first part of the main() function defines an array emps that contains four Employee elements, followed by the variable empPtr that is a pointer to a variable of type Employee. The next section initializes arrays for first names, last names, and titles.

The next section contains three loops. The first loop assigns values to all the fields of the elements of the emps array, using code that you saw in Listing 7.6. The second loop displays all the values of the Employee elements using a "dot" syntax, whereas the third loop performs the same task using the "arrow" syntax (shown in Listing 7.7).

Compile the code in Listing 7.8 and launch the executable and you will see the following output:

```
First name:   John
Last name:    Smith
Title:        Sales
Employee id: 1000

First name:   Jane
Last name:    Jones
Title:        Marketing
Employee id: 2000

First name:   Steve
Last name:    Edwards
Title:        Development
Employee id: 3000

First name:   John
Last name:    Anderson
Title:        Support
Employee id: 4000
// some output omitted for brevity
```

THE STRFTIME() AND STRPTIME() FUNCTIONS WITH DATES (OPTIONAL)

This section contains date-specific functionality that is significantly more involved the previous code samples that contain built-in C functions. If you do not plan to use dates in your C programs, feel free to skip this section with no loss of continuity (and perhaps return to this section at another point in time).

In C you can convert a date and time to a string using the strftime() function, and you can convert a string to a formatted time using the strptime() function, both of which are illustrated in Listing 7.9.

LISTING 7.9: DateTimeString.c

```
#include <stdio.h>
#include <locale.h>
#include <time.h>

int main()
{
    char buf[100];
    time_t t;
    struct tm *timeptr, result;

    setlocale(LC_ALL,"/QSYS.LIB/EN_US.LOCALE");
    t = time(NULL);

    timeptr = localtime(&t);
    strftime(buf,sizeof(buf), "%a %m/%d/%Y %r", timeptr);
```

```
if(strptime(buf, "%a %m/%d/%Y %r",&result) == NULL)
{
    printf("\nstrptime failed\n");
}
else
{
    printf("tm_hour:   %d\n",result.tm_hour);
    printf("tm_min:    %d\n",result.tm_min);
    printf("tm_sec:    %d\n",result.tm_sec);
    printf("tm_mon:    %d\n",result.tm_mon);
    printf("tm_mday:   %d\n",result.tm_mday);
    printf("tm_year:   %d\n",result.tm_year);
    printf("tm_yday:   %d\n",result.tm_yday);
    printf("tm_wday:   %d\n",result.tm_wday);
}

char s[100];
int rc;
time_t temp;
struct tm *timeptr2;

temp = time(NULL);
timeptr2 = localtime(&temp);

rc = strftime(s,sizeof(s),
        "Today is %A, %b %d.\nTime:   %r", timeptr2);
printf("%d characters written.\n%s\n",rc,s);

return 0;
}
```

Listing 7.9 starts with three #include statements, two of which are necessary for date-related functionality. The next section contains the main() function that declares a character buffer buf of length 100, followed by the variable t of type time_t, and the variables timeptr and result that are pointers to a C struct whose data type is tm. The next code section sets the locale via the function and initializes t as the current time.

Then the timeptr variable is initialized as the local time by invoking the C built-in localtime() function, with the address of the variable t as an argument. The next statement invokes the built-in strftime() C function in order to format the local date with via the specified format string.

The next section of code invokes the built-in strptime C function to assign a value to the result variable. If this fails, an error message is displayed; otherwise, the various attributes (e.g., hour, minute, second, and so forth) of the local date are displayed. The output from Listing 7.9 is here:

```
tm_hour:   13
tm_min:    51
tm_sec:    43
tm_mon:    2
tm_mday:   2
tm_year:   114
```

```
tm_yday:  0
tm_wday:  0
43 characters written.
Today is Sunday, Mar 02.
Time:  01:55:07 PM
```

SINGLY LINKED LISTS IN C (OPTIONAL)

If you are unfamiliar with linked lists, you can treat this section as optional, and perhaps return to this section after you have learned about linked lists.

As you have seen, the preceding section uses an array of C structs to keep track of employees. However, if you have an unknown number of employees, you can replace an array with a linked list in order to dynamically add each new employee to the linked list.

In order to simplify the code, the only data value in the C struct is an integer field that represents an employee id. After you have read the code sample, feel free to modify the C struct to include other relevant fields.

Listing 7.10 displays the contents of SLinkedList.c that illustrates how to create a singly linked list in C, where each element in the singly linked list is a C struct that contains an integer field and a forward pointer to an employee element. The C struct also contains a "commented out" previous pointer to an employee field, which is necessary if you want to create a doubly linked list.

LISTING 7.10: SLinkedList.c

```c
#include <stdio.h>
#include <stdlib.h>

struct emp {
   int x;
   struct emp *next;
//struct emp *prev;
};

int main()
{
    int empIdValues[] = {2000, 1000, 5000, 8000, 7500};
    int count = sizeof(empIdValues)/sizeof(empIdValues[0]);

    // the root emp is the first emp
    struct emp *root;

    // current emp and a new emp
    struct emp *currNode, *aNode;

    root = malloc( sizeof(struct emp) );
    root->x = empIdValues[0];
    root->next = NULL;
    currNode = root;

    for(int i=1; i<count; i++)
    {
```

```
        aNode = malloc( sizeof(struct emp) );
        aNode->x = empIdValues[i];
        aNode->next = NULL;
        currNode->next = aNode;
        currNode = aNode;
    }

    currNode = root;
    if(currNode != 0)
    {
        int idx = 1;
        while(currNode)
        {
            printf("Employee %d has id: %d\n", idx,
currNode->x);
            currNode = currNode->next;
            ++idx;
        }
    }

    return 0;
}
```

Listing 7.10 defines an emp C struct that contains an integer field, a pointer to an emp struct called prev, and a pointer to an emp C struct called next. This structure keeps track of the ID of an employee, and a pointer to the previous employee as well as the next employee (when they exist). The data fields in a real application would be much more extensive, but this example contains minimal information because it's easier to understand the code. The output from launching the C program in Listing 7.10 is here:

```
Employee 1 has id: 2000
Employee 2 has id: 1000
Employee 3 has id: 5000
Employee 4 has id: 8000
Employee 5 has id: 7500
```

As mentioned earlier, the definition of the emp C struct contains an additional pointer called prev that is a pointer to the previous employee (except for the root node). Thus, each node has a previous and a next pointer, which is a doubly linked list.

If you wish, you can extend the code in Listing 7.9 in order to implement a doubly linked list. If you are really ambitious, you can modify the code in Listing 7.9 in order to create other data structures in C, such as circular lists, stacks, queues, and trees.

UNIONS IN C

C provides the union data type that enables you to store different data types in the same memory location. Although you can define a C union with multiple members, only one member "at a time" can contain an actual value. The member that contains a value can change repeatedly during the execution of a program, but there is exactly one—at any given point in time—that contains a value.

The following example shows you how to use the C union keyword to define a C union data type:

```
union MyData
{
    int i;
    float f;
    char str[10];
} myunion;
```

The memory allocated to a C union equals the size of the largest member of the union. Thus, the MyData type requires 10 bytes because the str element occupies 10 bytes.

Listing 7.11 displays the contents of Unions.c that illustrates how construct a C union that contains an integer, a float value, and a character string.

LISTING 7.11: Unions.c

```
#include <stdio.h>
#include <string.h>

union MyData
{
    int i;
    float f;
    char str[10];
};

int main()
{
    union MyData mydata;

    printf("Memory allocated to mydata:
%d\n",sizeof(mydata));

    return 0;
}
```

Listing 7.11 defines the variable Data whose datatype is a C union, followed by the main() function that defines the variable myData whose data type is MyData and then displays the size of myData via a printf() statement.

The output from launching the C program in Listing 7.10 is here:

```
Memory allocated to mydata: 4 4 10
```

COMBINING A UNION AND A STRUCT IN C

You can create a custom data type in C that combines a C union and a C struct. Listing 7.12 displays the contents of Vector.c that defines a 3D vector (as a custom C union) that also contains a 2D vector (which is defined as a C struct).

LISTING 7.12: Vector.c

```c
#include <stdio.h>
#include <math.h>

// a 2D vector:
typedef struct {
    double x, y;
} vector2D;

// a 3D vector:
typedef struct {
    union {
        struct {
            double x, y;
        };
        vector2D v2;
    };
    double z;
} vector3D;

double length2D (vector2D v){
    return sqrt(v.x*v.x + v.y*v.y);
}

double length3D (vector3D v){
    return sqrt(v.x*v.x + v.y*v.y + v.z*v.z);
}

int main()
{
    vector3D v = {.x=5, .y=8, .z=4};
    printf("Vector v:    (%f,%f,%f)\n", v.x,v.y,v.z);
    printf("Magnitude:  %g\n", length3D(v));
    double projected = length2D(v.v2);
    printf("Projection: length of %g\n", projected);

    return 0;
}
```

Listing 7.12 defines the C struct vector2D that represents a two-dimensional point, followed by the C struct vector3D that contains a union data type followed by the variable z with data type double.

The next section of code defines the function length2D that computes the length of a 2D vector, which is the square root of the inner product of a vector with itself. The next function is length3D that computes the length of a 3D vector (which is also the square root of the inner product of a vector with itself).

The final portion of Listing 7.12 is the main() function that initializes the vector v of type vector3D, followed by printf() statements to display its components and its length. The next code block initializes the vector projected, which is a 2D vector that is derived from v via the component v.v2, and then the length of the vector projected is displayed. The output from launching the code in Listing 7.12 is here:

```
Vector v:    (5.000000,8.000000,4.000000)
Magnitude:   10.247
Projection: length of 9.43398
```

BITFIELDS IN C

Bitfields in C are well-suited to C struct data types that contain variables with true/false values. For instance, consider the following C struct definition:

```
struct

{
  unsigned int validDay;
  unsigned int validMonth;
} dateInfo;
```

The preceding C struct requires 8 bytes of memory even though the values are either 0 or 1. Alternatively, the following C bitfield definition is more compact:

```
struct
{
  unsigned int validDay: 1;
  unsigned int validMonth: 1;
} dateInfo;
```

On a typical system where an int is 32 bits, the previous C struct uses 4 bytes for the dateInfo variable, and 2 bits of memory for its elements. If you specify up to 32 bit values, the dateInfo variable requires 4 bytes. However, if you specify between 33 and 63 bit values, the dateInfo variable requires 8 bytes (you can no doubt see the pattern here).

Now let's look at Listing 7.13 that displays the contents of Bitfields.c to illustrate how to define bitfields in C.

LISTING 7.13: Bitfields.c

```
#include <stdio.h>
#include <string.h>

// define simple structure
struct
{
  unsigned int widthValidated;
  unsigned int heightValidated;
} status1;
```

```
// define a structure with bit fields
struct
{
  unsigned int widthValidated : 1;
  unsigned int heightValidated : 1;
} status2;

int main()
{
    printf("Memory size occupied by status1:
%d\n",sizeof(status1));
    printf("Memory size occupied by status2:
%d\n",sizeof(status2));

    return 0;
}
```

Listing 7.13 contains two C structs called status1 and status2, where the former specifies that widthValidated and heightValidated are of type unsigned int, and the latter initializes widthValidated and heightValidated with the value 1.

The output from launching the C program in Listing 7.13 is here:

```
Memory size of status1: 8
Memory size of status2: 4
```

DISPLAY ENVIRONMENT VARIABLES IN C

When you launch a C program, you can determine the value of variables in the current environment. You can also assign values to variables in the current environment. This section and the following section contain examples of how this can be done using the C functions getenv() and putenv().

Listing 7.14 displays the contents of PrintEnvVars.c that illustrates how to use the getenv() method in order to find the variables (and their values) in the current command shell where you launched the binary executable PrintEnvVars.

LISTING 7.14: PrintEnvVars.c

```
#include <stdlib.h>
#include <stdio.h>

int main(int argc, char **argv)
{
    char *pathvar;

    pathvar = getenv("PATH");
    printf("pathvar=%s",pathvar);
}
```

Listing 7.14 is straightforward: the `main()` function contains the built-in C function `getenv()` that is involved with the string `PATH`. The result of invoking `getenv()` is the value of the `PATH` environment variable, which is assigned to the character pointer `pathvar`. The last line of code in the `main()` function is the `printf()` function that displays the value of the `PATH` environment variable. The output from compiling and executing the code in Listing 7.14 is here:

```
pathvar=/Users/ocampesato/jython2.5.2:/Users/ocampesato/
anaconda/bin:/opt/local/bin:/Users/ocampesato/android-sdk-
mac_86/platform-tools:/Users/ocampesato/android-sdk-mac_86/
tools:/Users/ocampesato/apache-maven-3.1.1/bin:/usr/local/
bin:/Users/ocampesato/xalan-j_2_7_1:/Users/ocampesato/lua-
5.1.4/src:/Users/ocampesato/.rvm/bin:/Users/ocampesato/
mongoose:/Users/ocampesato/android-ndk-r4b:/usr/local/
bin:/usr/local/sbin:/usr/local/mysql/bin:/Applications/
XAMPP/xamppfiles/bin:/Users/ocampesato/phantomjs/bin:.:/
Users/ocampesato/anaconda/bin:/Library/Frameworks/Python.
framework/Versions/3.3/bin:/opt/local/bin:/opt/local/sbin:/
usr/bin:/bin:/usr/sbin:/sbin:/usr/local/bin:/usr/local/
CrossPack-AVR/bin:/usr/local/git/bin:/Users/ocampesato/.
rvm/bin:/Users/ocampesato/gradle-1.9/bin:/usr/local/go/
bin:/Applications/Xcode.app/Contents/Developer/Toolchains/
XcodeDefault.xctoolchain/usr/bin:/Users/ocampesato/gyp-
read-only:/Users/ocampesato/depot_tools:/Users/ocampesato/
hadoop-1.1.0/bin:/Users/ocampesato/.local/bin:/Users/
ocampesato/PebbleSDK-2.0-BETA5/binoswald-campesatos-
macbook:manuscript
```

SET ENVIRONMENT VARIABLES IN C

Listing 7.15 displays the contents of `SetEnvVars.c` that illustrates how to use the `putenv()` function in order to set ("put") a variable and its value in the current environment.

LISTING 7.15: SetEnvVars.c

```c
#include <stdlib.h>
#include <stdio.h>

int main(int argc, char **argv)
{
    char *pathvar;

    pathvar = getenv("PATH");
    printf("The current path is: %s\n\n", pathvar);

    if (-1 == putenv("PATH=/:/home/userid"))
    {
        printf("putenv failed \n");
        return EXIT_FAILURE;
    }
```

```
pathvar = getenv("PATH");
printf("The new path is: %s\n", pathvar);

    return 0;
}
```

Listing 7.15 reads the value of the PATH environment variable whereas Listing 7.14 sets the value of an environment variable. In fact, Listing 7.14 starts by invoking the getenv() function to read the value of the PATH environment variable and then invokes the built-in C function putenv() to assign a new value to the PATH variable. Notice the conditional logic: if the putenv() command fails, an error message is displayed.

The last portion of the main() function invokes the getenv() function again and displays the result, just to confirm that the PATH variable was updated correctly. The output (truncated for brevity) from compiling and executing the code in Listing 7.15 is here:

```
The current path is: /opt/spark/bin:/Users/owner/mongodb-
osx-x86_64-3.4.2/bin:/Users/owner/anaconda2/bin:
The new path is: /:/home/userid
```

Keep in mind that after the program finishes execution, the PATH variable will retain its initial value (i.e., the change is temporary).

STORAGE CLASS SPECIFIERS IN C

There are 5 storage class specifiers in C:

```
auto
extern
static
register
_Thread_local
```

The auto storage specifier indicates a variable has automatic storage duration. This is rarely used since it is the default. The extern keyword has to do with external linkage and is primarily used when declaring global variables in a header file. The static keyword has different meanings depending on context. It may declare a variable with static storage duration, which means its value persists over multiple invocations of a function. It may also declare a variable to have internal linkage.

The _Thread_local storage class is useful in multithreaded programming and declares a variable that has a different value for each thread. The register keyword used to be a hint to the compiler that a particular variable is used frequently and should be placed in a processor register for fast access. Compiler optimization has improved a great deal since the beginning of C and modern compilers simply ignore the register hint.

Some examples of using these C specifiers are:

```
register int i;    // i is an int, register keyword
                   // probably ignored
extern int j;      // declaration for j, j must be defined
                   // elsewhere
```

```
static int k = 0;      // variable k only visible in this
                       // translation unit
_Thread_local m = 5;   // m has a different instance in each
                       // thread

void f() {
    int n = 2;         // initialized to 2 every function
                       // call
    auto int m = 2;    // same as above, auto is the default
    static int o = 3;  // set to 3 on the first function call
}
```

HOW WRITE COMPLEX CODE WITH POINTERS

This facetiously titled section is intended to show you the type of code that is better to avoid because it's easy to make a mistake. Listing 7.16 displays the contents of DontDoThis.c that illustrates how to use the putenv() function in order to set ("put") a variable and its value in the current environment.

LISTING 7.16: DontDoThis.c

```c
#include <stdlib.h>

int main()
{
    // a data value and an array
    int value, array[10];

    // point to the first element
    int *arrptr = &array[0];
    printf("arrptr: %d\n", arrptr);

    // get element #0 from arrptr
    value = *arrptr++;
    printf("value1: %d\n", value);

    value = *++arrptr;
    printf("value2: %d\n", value);

    // get element #1 from arrptr
    value = ++*arrptr;
    printf("value3: %d\n", value);
}
```

Although the code in Listing 7.16 is syntactically correct, even experienced C programmers can inadvertently reference the memory location of a pointer instead of the contents of a pointer (a very common occurrence).

Launch the compiled code from Listing 7.16 and you will see the following output:

```
arrptr: 1560138064
value1: 280822976
value2: 0
```

```
value3: 1
```

As another example, consider the following code block that uses pointers in order to copy a string from the source (q) to the destination (p):

```
void copy_string(char *p, char *q) {
    while (*p++ = *q++);
}
```

Although it's possible to determine the purpose of the preceding code block, the following longer—yet equivalent—code is much easier to understand, maintain, and debug:

```
void copy_string(char *dest, char *source)
{
  while (1) {
    *dest = *source;

    // Exit if we copied the end of string
    if (*dest == '\0') return;

    ++source;
    ++dest;
  }
}
```

Notice that the if statement and the return statement are on the same line. In this example, the code is so straightforward that there's no possibility of confusion, which shows you that there can be exceptions to rules regarding code syntax.

ERROR HANDLING IN C

Although C does not provide direct support for error handling, you can determine the results of program execution via return values. Recall that the main() function in C programs has a return type of int, which means that you can return different values to indicate different results for the program execution.

The errno Global Variable

Most C function calls return either -1 or NULL in the event of an error, and set an error code via the global variable errno. Thus, you can check the value of this variable to determine how to proceed, based on the value of this variable. In case you're interested, various error codes are defined in <error.h> header file.

The perror() and strerror() Functions

The C programming language provides perror() and strerror() functions to display the text message associated with errno.

The `perror()` function displays the string you pass to it, followed by a colon, a space, and then the textual representation of the current `errno` value. For example, if your C program does not find a particular directory, the following message is displayed:

```
Error: No such file or directory
```

The `strerror()` function returns a pointer to the textual representation of the current `errno` value, and the output is similar to the output of the `perror()` function.

How to Exit from an Error

Keep in mind the following behavior: a C program that attempts a *floating point division by zero* is a runtime error, whereas an *integer division by zero* is undefined. The solution involves checking the value of the denominator before performing the division. Listing 7.17 displays the contents of `DivByZero.c` that illustrates how to prevent division by zero, along with a suitable text message.

LISTING 7.17: DivByZero.c

```c
#include <stdio.h>
#include <stdlib.h>

int main()
{
   int dividend = 20;
   int divisor = 5;
   int quotient;

   if( divisor == 0){
      fprintf(stderr, "Division by zero: exiting
program\n");
      exit(EXIT_FAILURE);
   }

   quotient = dividend / divisor;
   fprintf(stderr, "Value of quotient : %d\n", quotient );

   exit(EXIT_SUCCESS);
}
```

Listing 7.17 contains a `main()` function that initializes three integer-valued variables, followed by conditional logic that checks the value of the variable `divisor`.

Notice that the program with a value of `EXIT_SUCCESS` in case of success, where `EXIT_SUCCESS` is a macro, and exits with a status `EXIT_FAILURE` in case of an error.

One other detail: The C standard does not require any particular value for EXIT_SUCCESS and EXIT_FAILURE. The only requirement is that they must be defined and their value must be representable in an int.

Launch the compiled code in Listing 7.16 and you will see the following result:

```
Value of quotient : 4
```

The next section briefly discusses system calls in C, which is definitely an advanced topic. However, there are two code samples that are within your grasp, and they provide a gentle introduction to this topic.

SYSTEM CALLS IN C (OPTIONAL)

This topic is the final topic of this book, and arguably the most complex. This section provided an extremely brief description of system calls so that you will be aware of their existence and their purpose. This section also contains a very simple example of a C program that makes a system call.

Removing a File

Listing 7.18 displays the contents of SystemDeleteFile.c that illustrates how to invoke the unlink() command to delete a file.

LISTING 7.18: SystemDeleteFile.c

```c
#include <stdio.h>
#include <unistd.h>
#include <sys/syscall.h>

int main()
{
    char *filename = "text.txt";

    if (unlink("text.txt") == -1)
    {
        printf("File %s does not exist\n", filename);
    }
    else
    {
        printf("Successfully removed file %s\n", filename);
    }

    return 0;
}
```

Listing 7.18 contains a main() function that initializes the variable filename with the value text.txt. The next portion of code is conditional logic that invokes the built-in C function unlink() in order to delete the file text.txt. If the command fails, a suitable message is displayed. If the result is successful, a different message is displayed.

Now create a file called text.txt in the directory that contains file SystemDeleteFile.c. Compile this code and invoke the binary executable and you will see the following output:

```
Successfully removed file text.txt
```

Invoke this command again and this time you will see a different message:

```
File text.txt does not exist
```

Listing the Files in a Directory

Listing 7.19 displays the contents of SystemForkExec.c that illustrates how to use the fork() and exec() system calls to create a new process that lists the contents of a directory. Keep in mind that the fork() and exec() system calls are not part of the C language, and they are only available on systems that support the POSIX standard.

LISTING 7.19: SystemForkExec.c

```c
#include <stdio.h>
#include <unistd.h>
#include <sys/wait.h>

int main()
{
   char * ls_args[] = { "/bin/ls" , "-l", NULL};

   int pid = fork();

   if(pid == 0) // the child
   {
      execv(ls_args[0], ls_args);
   }
   else if(pid > 0) // the parent
   {
      // wait for the child to complete
      wait(NULL);
   }
   else
   {
      printf("Error: negative process ID\n");
   }

   exit(0);
}
```

Listing 7.19 starts with several #include statements that are required in order to execute the fork() and exec() system calls. The next section contains the main() function that initializes a character pointer to an array with three elements: the full path to the Unix ls command, the option to be used with the ls command, and the value NULL.

Next, the `fork()` function is invoked and the result is used to initialize the value of the integer `pid`. The key point to remember: if `pid` is zero, then we are in the child process; if `pid` is positive, then we are in the parent process; any other value for `pid` is an error (i.e., the `fork()` command failed).

The preceding scenarios are captured via conditional logic, where appropriate messages are displayed. The output from launching the code in Listing 7.19 is here:

```
-rwxr-xr-x  1 owner  staff  8560 Jul 24 19:22 SystemForkExec
-rw-r--r--  1 owner  staff     0 Jul 24 19:22 a
-rw-r--r--  1 owner  staff     0 Jul 24 19:22 b
-rw-r--r--  1 owner  staff     0 Jul 24 19:22 c
```

The binary executable `SystemForkExec` was invoked in a directory that contains the binary executable and the three files a, b, and c (all of size 0).

DEFINING CUSTOM FUNCTIONS IN MULTIPLE FILES (OPTIONAL)

This section shows you how to define custom functions in two C files and then include them in the compilation to create a single executable.

Listing 7.20, Listing 7.21, and Listing 7.22 display the contents of the files `FindChar2.h`, `FindChar2.c`, and `FindMain2.c`, which are compiled into one binary executable called `FindMain2`.

LISTING 7.20: FindChar2.h

```c
#include <ctype.h>
#include <stdio.h>

void findChar(char str[], char c);
```

Listing 7.20 is a very short header file: it contains two header files and the function prototype for the function `findChar()`.

LISTING 7.21: FindChar2.c

```c
#include <ctype.h>
#include <stdio.h>

void findChar(char str[], char c)
{
    int matchCount = 0;

    printf("String: %s\n",str);
    printf("Char:   %c\n",c);

    for(int i=0; str[i]; i++)
    {
        if(str[i] == c)
        {
            printf("Match in position: %d\n",i);
            ++matchCount;
```

```
        }
    }

    printf("Count:    %d\n\n",matchCount);
}
```

Listing 7.21 contains the implementation details of the function findChar()
that you saw in a code sample in Chapter 3.

LISTING 7.22: FindMain2.c

```
#include "FindChar2.h"

int main()
{
    char str1[] = "pasta";
    findChar(str1, 'a');

    char str2[] = "New York City";
    findChar(str2, 'k');

    char str3[] = "California";
    findChar(str3, 'z');

    return (0);
}
```

Listing 7.22 contains a local header file called FindChar2.h (i.e., it's not part
of the C language), followed by a main() function. Notice that the main()
function defines three strings and invokes the findChar() function (defined in
FindChar2.c) three times.

The C programs FindChar2.c and FindMain2.c need to be specified in
the compilation step involving gcc, as shown here:

```
# do not change the order of the next two lines:
gcc -std=c11 -Wall -c FindChar2.c
gcc -std=c11 FindChar2.o FindMain2.c -o FindMain2
```

The output of the preceding code snippet is the binary executable FindMain2,
and the output from launching FindMain2 is here:

```
String: pasta
Char:    a
Match in position: 1
Match in position: 4
Count:   2

String: New York City
Char:    k
Match in position: 7
Count:   1

String: California
Char:    z
```

The preceding example is manageable because there are only three files involved, which you can specify from the command line when you invoke gcc. However, a C program can have multiple dependencies involving dozens of files, and keeping track of them (along with dependencies on header files and custom libraries) can quickly become untenable. One solution involves the make utility, which is discussed in the Appendix.

STANDARD HEADER FILES AND LIBRARIES

As you have seen throughout the code samples in this book, C programs invariably require standard header files in order to compile them into object files, along with standard libraries in order to perform the link step that creates an executable file.

Note that /usr/include is used on Unix and Unix-like systems only, whereas Windows compilers have their "include" files somewhere in the installation directory.

Standard Header Files (Unix-like Systems)

On Unix-like systems, the directory /usr/include contains various "header" files, some of which are displayed below (from a Macbook Pro):

```
AppleTextureEncoder.h
AssertMacros.h
Availability.h
AvailabilityInternal.h
AvailabilityMacros.h
Block.h
CommonCrypto
ConditionalMacros.h
MacTypes.h
[files omitted for brevity]
wordexp.h
xar
xattr_flags.h
xlocale
xlocale.h
xpc
zconf.h
zlib.h
```

The /usr/include directory contains the various "header" files that are included in every C program in this book. You will see an example in the next section. In addition, you can create custom header files that you can place in your projects and then reference them in your C programs.

You can include a header file in a C program by placing the following type of statement at the beginning of a C program:

```
#include <stdio.h>
```

If you have a custom header file called `mystdio.h` that is located in the same directory as your C program, you can reference this header file with the following syntax:

```
#include "mystdio.h"
```

Commonly Used Header Files

The following list contains commonly used C header files, along with a brief explanation of their purpose:

```
<ctype.h>  defines character manipulation routines
<math.h>   defines mathematical routines
<stdio.h>  defines I/O routines
<stdlib.h> defines number conversion, storage allocation and
similar tasks
<stdarg.h> defines libraries to handle routines with
variable numbers of arguments
<string.h> defines string manipulation routines
<time.h>   defines time-manipulation routines
In addition, the following header files exist:
<assert.h> defines diagnostic routines
<float.h>  defines constants of the float type
<limits.h> defines constants of the int type
<setjmp.h> defines non-local function calls
<signal.h> defines signal handlers
```

If necessary, you can perform an online search to find more information about these header files.

Standard Libraries

The directory `/usr/lib` contains various libraries, some of which are displayed below:

```
PN548_API.dylib
PN548_HAL_OSX.dylib
PN548_OSX.dylib
bundle1.o
charset.alias
cron
crt1.10.5.o
crt1.10.6.o
[files omitted for brevity]
rpcsvc
ruby
sasl2
sqlite3
ssh-keychain.dylib
```

The two main types of libraries are static and dynamic, both of which are used in this book. The Appendix shows you how to reference header files and libraries in a Makefile that specifies various dependencies for compiling C code and creating binary files.

SUMMARY

In this chapter you learned about C `structs`, and saw examples of creating nested C `structs`, pointers to C `structs`, and arrays of C `structs`. You also saw how to define C unions and C bitfields. Then you learned about header files, and how to define and reference local header files in a C program. Then you learned basic information about system calls and how to use the `unlink()`, `fork()`, and `exec()` system commands. Finally, you learned about the standard location for commonly used C header files and C libraries (typically in `make` files) in C programs.

THE MAKE UTILITY

This Appendix discusses the make utility that can help you manage C applications that have multiple dependencies. The make utility excels in managing projects that involve recompiling C programs (based on their date of modification), creating object files, updating libraries, and integrating other artifacts. Although the examples in this Appendix are for C programs, the make utility works just as well for C++ projects.

The first part of this Appendix starts by describing the make utility and a Makefile, and then briefly discusses Unix commands for managing object files and libraries, such as the ar command and the ranlib command. You will also learn how to use the nm command for C programs that will help you find symbol definitions.

The second part of this Appendix delves into the make utility, which is the bulk of the material in this Appendix. You will learn how to use the make utility with some simple examples, macros in makefiles, and how to create multiple executable files.

The third part shows you how to specify header files and library files in a makefile, and how to define nested makefiles. The remaining portion of this Appendix contains a miscellaneous assortment of other features of the make utility.

WHAT IS THE MAKE UTILITY?

The make utility is a binary executable that reads the contents of a text-based "makefile" in order to execute commands. The make utility searches (in the current directory) for a file named Makefile and if this file does not exist, it searches for a file named makefile. If neither file exists, then the make utility fails with this message:

```
make: *** No targets specified and no makefile found.  Stop.
```

As you will see later in this Appendix, you can use the `-f` switch for the `make` utility in order to specify a makefile with a different name. In this Appendix the term "makefile" will refer to the file `Makefile` ("big Make") as the default file.

What is in **Makefile**?

The file `Makefile` typically contains so-called rules for executing various commands, such as compiling out-of-date C programs. Without going into the syntax rules (we'll discuss them later), here are the contents of a `Makefile` that contains a single rule for creating a binary executable called `hello`:

```
hello: HelloWorld.c
        gcc -Wall HelloWorld.c -o HelloWorld
```

Note that the second line in the preceding code snippet starts with a mandatory <tab> character that is not visible in this page.

You can also specify additional files that are not included by default during the compilation process. For instance you can specify custom "header" files (text files with a `.h` suffix), other object files (binary files with a `.o` suffix), or additional libraries (binary files with a `.a` or `.so` suffix) that are necessary for creating a binary executable.

The file `Makefile` can also contain rules that do not involve compilation, such as shell scripts and Unix commands. You can also create a "master" `Makefile` that contains rules that invoke the `make` utility using a `Makefile` located in a subdirectory. This is very useful, because you can subdivide a large project into a set of modules, where the code for each module is in a different subdirectory that contains a module-specific `Makefile`.

The next section discusses some useful commands (such as `ar`, `ranlib`, and `nm`) that you can specify in a `Makefile` target in order to operate compilation-related steps for your C programs.

USEFUL UNIX COMMANDS FOR LIBRARIES

Throughout this book you have used the `gcc` utility to create binary executable files from C programs. However, in mid-sized and larger projects, C applications often involve "assembling" multiple C files into a single binary file. Those C files are compiled into so-called object files, which are binary files with a ".o" extension.

The `ar` ("archive") command enables you to combine multiple ".o" files into a library file, which is a binary file with a ".a" extension (which are static libraries). In particular, the `ar` command enables you to add, remove, or update ".o" files in a library file.

Another very useful utility is the `nm` command for finding symbol definitions in ".o" files or library files. This utility helps you deal with "undefined symbol" errors that arise when you have not included the necessary object file or library that's required in order to create a binary executable. Generally you would use this utility from the command line and less frequently in a `Makefile`.

Examples of the `ar` Command

The following command creates a static library called `HelloWorld.a` that contains the object file `HelloWorld.o`:

```
ar -r HelloWorld.a HelloWorld.o
```

Add all the object files in the current directory to the library `HelloWorld.a` with this command:

```
ar -r HelloWorld.a *.o
```

The following command updates `HelloWorld.a` with the contents of `HelloWorld.o`:

```
ar -rcsHelloWorld.aHelloWorld.o
```

An example of using the `ar` command in a `Makefile` is here:

```
mylib.a: class.o
    ar -r mylib.a class.o
```

In the preceding snippet, the "r" switch means insert the file `class.o` into the archive `mylib.a`. Search online for examples of other switches for the `ar` command.

The `ranlib` Command

Every archive library contains a table of contents that keeps track of the .o files in the library. The `ranlib` utility adds or updates the table of contents of archive libraries so that the link editor can link the library. In addition, the table of contents is an archive member at the beginning of the archive that indicates which symbols are defined in which library members.

The nm Command

The nm command displays the symbols that are defined or referenced in a static library. For example, suppose that the library `HelloWorld.a` contains the object file `HelloWorld.o`.

If you type the following command:

```
nm HelloWorld.a
```

The output will be something like this:

```
HelloWorld.a(HelloWorld.o):
0000000000000308 s EH_frame0
0000000000000030 s L_.str
0000000000000000 T _main
0000000000000320 S _main.eh
                 U _printf
```

```
HelloWorld.a(FindChar2.o):
0000000000000420 s EH_frame0
00000000000000c6 s L_.str
00000000000000d2 s L_.str1
00000000000000de s L_.str2
00000000000000f5 s L_.str3
0000000000000000 T _findChar
0000000000000438 S _findChar.eh
                 U _printf

HelloWorld.a(FindMain2.o):
0000000000000440 s EH_frame0
00000000000000c0 s L_main.str1
00000000000000c6 s L_main.str2
00000000000000d4 s L_main.str3
                 U ___stack_chk_fail
                 U ___stack_chk_guard
                 U _findChar
0000000000000000 T _main
0000000000000458 S _main.eh
```

The letter U in the second column in the preceding output indicates that the function specified on the right side of U is referenced in the associated .o file, and that its definition is located in a different archive library or object file.

SOME SIMPLE MAKEFILES

This section contains a makefile that does not involve any compilation of C programs. They contain simple rules that execute simple commands. Note that you must use the –f switch because of the non-standard filename.

Listing A.1 displays the contents of Simplemake that contains a top-level "target" called all. This target specifies three other targets for executing Unix commands.

LISTING A.1: Simplemake

```
all: hello now mymakefiles


hello:
        echo "hello world"; echo
now:
        @echo "now is 'date'"; echo
mymakefiles:
        @echo "mymakefiles: 'ls *akefile*'"; echo
```

Listing A.1 defines the target all that specifies the three targets called hello, now, and mymakefiles. Invoking the make utility by specifying the file Simplemake will cause all three targets to be invoked, simply by typing the following command:

```
make -f Simplemake
```

The output from my system is shown here:

```
echo "hello world"; echo
hello world

now is Wed May 23 22:50:28 PDT 2018

mymakefiles: Makefile
Makefile-ori
Makefile1
Makefile2
Makefile3
Makefile4
Makefile5
Makefile6
Makefile7
Makefile8
Makefile9
```

If you only want to invoke the first target, then type the following command:

```
make -f Simplemake hello
```
The output from my system is shown here:

```
echo "hello world"; echo
hello world
```

If you only want to invoke the second target, then type the following command:

```
make -f Simplemake now
```

The output from my system is shown here:

```
now is Wed May 23 22:50:28 PDT 2018
```

Finally, if you only want to invoke the third target, then type the following command:

```
make -f Simplemake mymakefiles
```

Keep in mind one thing: the preceding target will list the files containing the string `akefile`. Hence, this target will *not* list makefiles that do not match this pattern, such as `mymake`, `mymakefile`, `yourmakefile`, and so forth.

With the preceding example in mind, let's look at an example of a makefile that involves compiling a C program, as discussed in the next section.

A MAKEFILE FOR C PROGRAMS

Recall that Chapter 1 contains the C program `HelloWorld.c` that you compiled with the following command:

```
gcc HelloWorld.c -o HelloWorld
```

The equivalent functionality of the preceding command involves creating a simple target in a makefile, which is displayed in Listing A.2.

LISTING A.2: Makefile

```
hello: HelloWorld.c
        gcc HelloWorld.c -o HelloWorld
```

Listing A.2 defines the target `hello`, but you can use whatever name is convenient for you.

Now place the `Makefile` in Listing A.2 and the C program `HelloWorld.c` in the same directory, and then launch the `make` utility from the command line, just as you did in the previous section. Although no output is displayed, you will see the binary file `HelloWorld` appear in the same directory; launch this file and you will see the following output:

```
Hello World
```

A `Makefile` often contains multiple targets and can include other constructs such as macro definitions and also reference other makefiles. Keep in mind that the files that are specified on the right-side of the colon are the dependencies, which is `HelloWorld.c` in this example. The second line has a tab-based indentation that is required for any target in a makefile but is not visible in this example. If you use spaces instead of a tab, you will see the following type of error message when you invoke the `make` utility:

```
Makefile1:13: *** missing separator (did you mean TAB
instead of 8 spaces?).  Stop.
```

This is one of the most common errors that developers make when they create makefiles.

NOTE *The first character in a rule line must be a tab character.*

A very simple makefile with the preceding target is discussed in the next section.

BIG MAKE AND LITTLE MAKE

As you saw earlier in this Appendix, the file `Makefile` is called "big make" and the file makefile is called "little make." If you type make on the command line, it will search for "big make" and execute the first target in that makefile. If "big make" does not exist, the `make` utility searches for "little make" and execute the first target in that makefile.

For example, if the `hello` target is defined in either `Makefile` (such as the one in Listing A.2) or makefile, you can invoke that target as follows:

```
make hello
```

As a reminder, if `Makefile` and `makefile` do not exist and you invoke the preceding command, the following message is printed:

```
make: *** No rule to make target `hello'.  Stop.
```

A MakeFile with Macros

Listing A.3 displays the contents of `Makefile2` that contains two macro definitions and three targets, all of which create the binary executable `HelloWorld`.

LISTING A.3: Makefile2

```
CC=gcc
CFLAGS=-g -Wall

hello: HelloWorld.c
        gcc HelloWorld.c -o HelloWorld

hello2: HelloWorld.c
        gcc -g -Wall HelloWorld.c -o HelloWorld

hello3: HelloWorld.c
        $(CC) $(CFLAGS) HelloWorld.c -o HelloWorld
```

Invoke the first target with the following command:

```
make hello -f Makefile2
```

Invoke the second target with the following command:

```
make hello2 -f Makefile2
```

Invoke the third target with the following command:

```
make hello3 -f Makefile2
```

The result of the three preceding targets is the creation of the binary executable `HelloWorld`. However, note that only the rule for `hello3` refers to $(CC), which means that there will be no change if you alter the value of CC and run the `hello` target.

In case you're wondering, one advantage to using macros is that you can replace their definitions in a single location without modifying any of the targets or their dependencies. For example, Listing A.3 defines the GCC macro with the value of gcc; however, you can replace gcc with another utility, such as g++ (if it's available on your system). Try making this change and execute the same command as above:

```
make hello -f Makefile2
```

The result is the same, which is the creation of the binary executable `HelloWorld`.

There are some standard targets available in makefiles, some of which are shown in the next section.

A MAKEFILE WITH STANDARD TARGETS

Listing A.4 displays the contents of `Makefile3` that contains three macro definitions and three targets, all of which create the binary executable `HelloWorld`.

LISTING A.4: Makefile3

```
CC=gcc
CFLAGS=-g -Wall
RM=/bin/rm

# only the 'hello' target
all: hello

# just the 'hello' target
hello: HelloWorld.c
        $(CC) $(CFLAGS) HelloWorld.c -o HelloWorld

# what to remove
clean:
        $(RM) HelloWorld
```

Listing A.4 contains only the target `hello:` the targets `hello2` and `hello3` have been removed because they do not serve any useful purpose.

As another illustration, Listing A.5 displays the contents of `Makefile4` that fully "generalizes" the executables that are referenced.

LISTING A.5: Makefile4

```
CC=gcc
CFLAGS=-g -Wall
RM=/bin/rm -f
MAKE=/usr/bin/make
ECHO=echo

# only the 'hello' target
all: hello

# just the 'hello' target
hello: HelloWorld.c
        $(ECHO) "Creating HelloWorld in target hello..."
        $(CC) $(CFLAGS) HelloWorld.c -o HelloWorld

# what to remove
clean:
        $(RM) HelloWorld
```

The initial portion of Listing A.5 contains macros for all the binary executables that are used in the targets, such as `gcc`, `rm`, `make`, and `echo`.

Command Line Switches for Makefiles

There are various switches that you can specify when you invoke the `make` utility. For example, you have already used the "`-f`" switch to specify the name of a makefile:

```
make -f Makefile1
```

The preceding command runs the commands from the first target in `Make-file1`, provided the dependent files are more recent than the target.

The "`-n`" switch displays the outcome of the execution of the `make` utility without actually executing a makefile:

```
make -f Makefile1
```

You can combine switches as shown here:

```
make -n -f Makefile1
```

As an illustration, suppose that `Makefile1` contains the following target:

```
hello: HelloWorld.c
        gcc HelloWorld.c -o HelloWorld
```

The following command invokes the target hello in `Makefile1`:

```
make -f Makefile1 hello
```

The previous code snippet causes an invocation of the `gcc` command in order to compile the C program `HelloWorld.c` and to create the executable `HelloWorld`.

HOW DO MAKEFILES WORK?

Since every file on the file system has a timestamp that indicates when the file was last modified, the make checks the timestamp of a file and its dependencies in order to determine whether a target must be invoked. In addition, when dependencies are checked, updates are performed recursively.

For example, if a C source code file has a timestamp that is more recent than its corresponding executable, then the associated target in the makefile is invoked, and the associated commands are executed.

In many cases the purpose of the makefile is to create an executable, and the associated target is often the first target in the makefile. For example, if `FindMain2` is the first target in a makefile, then make will execute the commands for the target `FindMain2`.

NOTE *By default "make" always runs the commands from the first target in the makefile, but not any of the commands in other targets.*

If you do not specify the "`-o`" switch the compiler will create the default executable whose name is `a.out`.

In general terms, a makefile contains one or more entries, where each entry consists of the following:

+a target (usually a file)

+its dependencies (the files that the target depends on)

+the commands to invoke (based on the target and dependencies)

Keep in mind that dependencies are transitive. For example, if A depends on B and B depends on C, then A depends on C. Examine your C programs to determine the dependencies for each file and then add the appropriate target to your makefile.

You can also use the `makedepend` program that analyzes the header files (".h") in your C programs in order to determine dependencies.

MULTIPLE SOURCE FILES AND THE MAKE UTILITY

The C programs in previous chapters do not have dependencies on other C programs. However, when dependencies exist on other C programs (written by you or someone else), you can define targets for those other C programs.

For example, suppose that the C program `main1.c` depends on the C programs `depend1.c` and `depend2.c`, whose contents are displayed in Listing A.6, Listing A.7, and Listing A.8, respectively.

https://www.thegeekstuff.com/2012/03/linux-nm-command/

LISTING A.6: main1.c

```
#include <stdio.h>
#include "depend1.h"
#include "depend2.h"

int main()
{
    printf("Hello from main1.c\n");
    depend1();
    depend2();
    return 0;
}
```

Listing A.6 includes two .h files that are in the same directory as `main1.c`: you can determine this fact because the include statements use double quotes ("") instead of angle (<>) brackets. Next, the `main()` function starts with a `printf()` statement, followed by an invocation of the functions `depend1()` and `depend2()`, neither of which is defined in this C program.

LISTING A.7: depend1.c

```
#include <stdio.h>

void depend1()
{
    printf("Hello from depend1.c\n");
```

}

Listing A.7 starts with the `main()` function that contains a single `printf()` statement that displays the name of the current file `depend1.c`. The only purpose of this statement is to help you see the flow of program execution.

LISTING A.8: depend2.c

```
#include <stdio.h>

void depend2()
{
    printf("Hello from depend2.c\n");
}
```

Listing A.8 starts with the `main()` function that contains a single `printf()` statement that displays the name of the current file `depend2.c`. The only purpose of this statement is to help you see the flow of program execution.

Listing A.9 displays the contents of the file `Makefile5` that specifies the required dependencies.

LISTING A.9: Makefile5

```
CC=gcc
CFLAGS=-g -Wall
RM=/bin/rm -f

OBJECTS = depend1.o depend2.o
HEADERS = depend1.h depend2.h

main1: $(OBJECTS) $(HEADERS)
        $(CC) $(CFLAGS) $(OBJECTS) HelloWorld.c -o
HelloWorld

depend1.o: depend1.c
        $(CC) -c depend1.c

depend2.o: depend2.c
        $(CC) -c depend2.c

clean:
        $(RM) main1 $(OBJECTS) 2>/dev/null
```

Listing A.9 contains several macros that you have seen in previous makefiles, along with the macros OBJECTS and HEADERS that specify a list of object files and header files, respectively.

The next portion of Listing A.9 defines the target `main1` that depends on the object files and the header files. The next pair of targets specify how to compile the source files `depend1.c` and `depend2.c` in order to generate the object files `depend1.o` and `depend2.o`, respectively.

The final target is a standard target for "cleaning" files, which in this case is the object files specified by $(OBJECTS) and the binary executable `main1`.

Note that if either depend1.c or depend2.c is modified, then that file is recompiled in order to create the corresponding object file, which in turn is included in the step for creating a new version of the binary executable main1.

Launch the make command with the -f switch as follows:

```
make -f Makefile5
```

Now launch the newly created executable:

```
./main1
```

The output is shown here:

```
Hello from main1.c
Hello from depend1.c
Hello from depend2.c
```

The next section shows you how to create a makefile that can handle multiple dependencies in a succinct manner.

MACROS FOR MULTIPLE C FILES

In Chapter 7, you used the following command in order to generate the binary executable FindMain2:

```
gcc -o FindMain2 FindChar2.c FindMain2.c
```

Listing A.10 displays the contents of Makefile6 with a FindMain2 as a target, which is generated when any of its dependencies are modified.

LISTING A.10: Makefile6

```
CC=gcc
CFLAGS=-g -Wall
RM=/bin/rm -f

EXEC = main1
SRC = $(EXEC).c depend1.c depend2.c
OBJ = $(SRC:.c=.o)
LIB = $(SRC:.c=.h)

all: $(EXEC)

# this target generates main1
$(EXEC): $(OBJ)
        $(CC) -o $@ $^ $(LDFLAGS) -lm

%.o: $.c $(LIB)
        $(CC) -o $@ -c $< $(CFLAGS)

clean:
        $(RM) main1 2>/dev/null
```

Listing A.10 starts with some familiar macro definitions, followed by the macros EXEC, SRC, OBJ, and LIB that are specific to the makefile in which these macros are defined.

The OBJ macro contains a rule that specifies how to generate object files ".o" from C source files. The LIB macro contains a rule that specifies how to determine the header files that are associated with C source files.

OTHER MACROS IN MAKEFILES

A macro is a simple string that has been assigned a value, after which you can use the string in a makefile target. The general syntax involves specifying a name and then assigning it a value, as shown here:

```
macroname = macrovalue
```

A macro bears some resemblance to a #define in C programs that you have seen in earlier chapters. Whenever the make command encounters a macro name, it substitutes the macro name with its defined value. In fact, an earlier makefile in this Appendix contains simple macros, as shown here:

```
CC=gcc
CFLAGS=-g -Wall
RM=/bin/rm

hello: HelloWorld.c
        $(CC) $(CFLAGS) HelloWorld.c -o HelloWorld
```

The preceding target uses parentheses to reference the value of macros, but you can also use curly braces. For example, you can use either $(CC) or ${CC}.

By convention a macro name contains a combination of upper case letters and underscores. In addition, you can specify more complex macros that involve multiple files. For example, suppose that the C file BigMain.c depends on the following object ("dot-oh") files: Sub1.o, Sub2.o, Sub3.o, and Sub4.o. You can define a macro that specifies these object files as follows:

```
OBJS = Sub1.o Sub2.o Sub3.o Sub4.o
```

The target in your makefile would look something like this (obviously there could be other dependencies as well):

```
BigMain: $(OBJS)
    $(CC) $(LFLAGS) $(OBJS) -o BigMain
```

A macro can be used as part of the definition of other macros. You can also place the continuation character backslash "\" (followed by a newline) in order to define a macro that spans more than one line.

Although it might not be readily apparent in short makefiles, macros become very convenient in large makefiles because they enable you to define "variables" that are substituted in the targets that reference them.

Some common macros for C programs are here:

CC is the name of the compiler

DEBUG is the debugging flag, which is typically just –g

LFLAGS specifies the flags required during the link step: -Wall instructs the compiler to print all warnings

CFLAGS specifies the flags for compiling and creating object files

You will notice that once a macro is defined, it can be used to define subsequent macros.

Since the makefiles in this Appendix are simple and short, there is limited value to using macros. Nevertheless, it's a good idea to develop the habit of using macros in makefiles, especially if they are likely to become more complex.

Automatic Variables

If you want to become really proficient with the make utility, you need to learn many of the variables that have a special significance in makefiles. Here is a short list of some supported variables, along with a short description of their purpose:

$@ is the file name of the target of a rule

$% is the target member name: if the target is foo.a(bar.o) then $% is bar.o and $@ is foo.a.

$< is the name of the first prerequisite

$? is the names of all the prerequisites that are newer than the target

$^ is the names of all the prerequisites

The make utility supports many other built-in variables, and you can perform an online search to find more information.

CREATING MULTIPLE EXECUTABLES IN A MAKEFILE

Sometimes you need to create multiple binary executable files, and the make utility enables you to specify the targets in a straightforward manner. Suppose that you need to create three executables called mybin1, mybin2, and mybin3, where each executable depends on its associated C program as well as the HelloWorld.c program.

Listing A.11 displays the contents of Makefile7 that illustrates how to specify the targets.

LISTING A.11: Makefile7

```
CC=gcc
CFLAGS=-g -Wall
RM=/bin/rm

# invokes targets mybin1, mybin2, and mybin3
all: mybin1 mybin2 mybin3

# 'mybin1' creates mybin1
```

```
mybin1: mybin1.o HelloWorld.o
        $(CC) $(CFLAGS) HelloWorld.c -o mybin1

# 'mybin2' creates mybin2
mybin2: mybin2.o HelloWorld.o
        $(CC) $(CFLAGS) HelloWorld.c -o mybin2

# 'mybin3' creates mybin3
mybin3: mybin3.o HelloWorld.o
        $(CC) $(CFLAGS) HelloWorld.c -o mybin3

# removes mybin1, mybin2, mybin3, and *.o files
clean:
        $(RM) mybin1 mybin2 mybin3 *.o
```

Listing A.11 starts with several macro definitions, followed by the `all` target that specifies the dependencies `mybin1`, `mybin2`, and `mybin3`, but there are no command line dependencies. As a result, the `make` utility attempts to build the most up-to-date versions of those files.

OTHER TYPES OF TARGETS IN A MAKEFILE

Thus far the targets in the sample makefiles involve creating object files or binary executables, but you can define other types of targets. For example, Listing A.12 displays the contents of `MakefileTar` that illustrates how to create a `tar` (**tape ar**chive) file and extract the contents of a `tar` file.

LISTING A.12: MakefileTar

```
TAR=/usr/bin/tar
CTFLAGS=-cvf
XTFLAGS=-xvf
TARFILE=mytar.tar

ctarfile:
        @echo "### Listing of C Programs:"
        @ls -l *.c
        @echo "### Creating tar file:"
        $(TAR) $(CTFLAGS) $(TARFILE) *.c

xtarfile:
        @echo "### Extracting tar file:"
        $(TAR) $(XTFLAGS) $(TARFILE)
```

Listing A.12 starts with several macro definitions, followed by two targets. The first target is `ctarfile`, which will display a long listing of the C programs in the current directory, and then create a tar file with those C programs.

The second target is `xtarfile`, which will perform the opposite of the `ctarfile` target: it extracts the contents of the tar file `mytar.tar` that was created in the `ctarfile` target.

The output from invoking the `ctarfile` target is here:

```
### Listing of C Programs:
-rw-r--r--  1 ocampesato  staff  2048 Jan 26 12:40 Hello2.c
-rw-r--r--  1 ocampesato  staff    83 Jan 19 21:30
HelloWorld.c
### Creating tar file:
/usr/bin/tar -cvf mytar.tar *.c
a Hello2.c
a HelloWorld.c
```

The output from invoking the `xtarfile` target is here:

```
### Extracting tar file:
/usr/bin/tar -xvf mytar.tar
x Hello2.c
x HelloWorld.c
```

SPECIFYING HEADERS AND LIBRARIES IN A MAKEFILE

You have seen several makefiles with targets that specify header files as dependencies. In addition, you can specify a header file using the "`-I`" prefix to a path-qualified directory, as shown here:

```
-I/usr/include
```

The preceding line enables the `make` utility to search user-specified directories for header files.

The `-I` option in the preceding line is actually passed to the compiler by the makefile; i.e., it is not passed on the command line to the `make` command. However, the `make` utility also supports a `-I` command which sets up a search path for makefiles. Note that the directory `/usr/include` is included by default, so it's unnecessary to specify this directory.

On the other hand, suppose you create the header file `mytime.h` that is located in the `/usr/local/include` directory. Then the following code snippet will enable the compiler to find `mytime.h` in the correct location:

```
-I/usr/local/include
```

The advantage of the preceding code snippet is that you won't need to explicitly reference the contents of this directory in your custom header files or custom C programs.

In addition, you can use the following switch in order to instruct the compiler to search the current directory for header files:

```
-I.
```

Yet another option involves specifying a directory—relative to the current directory:

```
CC=gcc
IDIR =../include
CFLAGS=-I$(IDIR)
```

Specifying Libraries

The `make` utility allows you to specify a library in a makefile in two ways.

The shorthand way involves 1) removing the "lib" prefix, 2) removing the suffix, and 3) specifying "-l" (lowercase l) as the prefix for whatever remains after performing steps #1 and #2.

For example, if you want to include the library `/usr/lib/libm.a` as part of the process of creating an executable, specify the string "-lm" in order to include this library.

The longer way of doing the same thing is to specify the full path to the library as part of the compilation step (preferably as a macro definition), as shown here:

```
-L/usr/lib/libm.a
```

DUMMY TARGETS IN A MAKEFILE

If you want to execute commands instead of creating a target, you can define a dummy target, which does not involve any files.

There are some common dummy targets used in makefiles:

```
make clean
make all
```

The "clean" target is typically used for removing files (such as object files and executables) from a directory. The removal of such files forces the makefile to recompile all the ".o" files.

INCLUDING A MAKEFILE IN ANOTHER MAKEFILE

Source code trees often have a separate makefiles in the main directories of the source code that handle the dependencies that are local to a given directory. A top-level makefile acts as the "master" makefile that contains targets for creating one or more executables.

Listing A.13 displays the contents of `BranchMakefile` that contains a target that will execute a target in `BranchMakefile` that is located in the branch subdirectory.

LISTING A.13: BranchMakefile

```
CC=gcc
CFLAGS=-g -Wall
RM=/bin/rm
MAKE=/usr/bin/make
BRANCH=./branch
ECHO=echo

# only the 'hello' target
all: hello

# 'hello' creates HelloWorld
hello: HelloWorld.c
        $(ECHO) top-level directory...
        $(CC) $(CFLAGS) HelloWorld.c -o HelloWorld
        $(ECHO) going to branch...
        cd $(BRANCH); $(MAKE) -f SubBranchMakefile goodbye

# 'Helloworld.o' creates HelloWorld.o
HelloWorld.o: HelloWorld.c
        $(CC) $(CFLAGS) -c HelloWorld.c

# removes HelloWorld and HelloWorld.o
clean:
        $(RM) HelloWorld HelloWorld.o
```

Listing A.13 starts with several macro definitions, followed by four targets. The first target is all, which depends on the target hello. The hello target prints a statement, compiles the file HelloWorld.o to create HelloWorld, and then prints another statement. The last step in this target execution involves navigating into a subdirectory and invoking the make utility with the -f switch to specify the makefile called BranchMakefile and the target goodbye.

The third target creates the object file HelloWorld.o, and the final target is the clean target that removes the files HelloWorld and HelloWorld.o.

LISTING A.14: SubBranchMakefile

```
CC=gcc
CFLAGS=-g -Wall
RM=/bin/rm

# 'goodbye' creates GoodbyeWorld
goodbye: GoodbyeWorld.c
        $(CC) $(CFLAGS) GoodbyeWorld.c -o GoodbyeWorld

# 'GoodbyeWorld.o' creates GoodbyeWorld.o
GoodbyeWorld.o: GoodbyeWorld.c
        $(CC) $(CFLAGS) -c GoodbyeWorld.c

# removes GoodbyeWorld and GoodbyeWorld.o
clean:
        $(RM) GoodbyeWorld GoodbyeWorld.o
```

Listing A.14 starts with several familiar macro definitions, followed by three targets whose syntax is also familiar to you. Note that the goodbye target in this makefile is invoked indirectly via one of the targets in the makefile in Listing A.13.

Now type the following command from the directory that contains the BranchMakefile in Listing A.13 (and *not* from the subdirectory):

```
make -f BranchMakefile
```

The output from the preceding command is here:

```
echo top-level directory...
top-level directory...
gcc -g -Wall HelloWorld.c -o HelloWorld
echo going to branch...
going to branch...
cd ./branch; /usr/bin/make -f BranchMakefile goodbye
gcc -g -Wall GoodbyeWorld.c -o GoodbyeWorld
```

Although the preceding example is somewhat artificial, you can see how to adapt the makefiles to handle multiple subdirectories containing source code for your project.

CREATING A LIBRARY ARCHIVE FROM OBJECT FILES

Listing A.15 displays the contents of Makefile8 that illustrates how to create a library containing a set of object files that are located in the current directory.

LISTING A.15 Makefile8

```
RM=/bin/rm -f
AR=/usr/bin/ar
MYLIB=mylib.a

# only the 'hello' target
all: lib

# create a library with .o files
lib: FindChar2.o FindMain2.o HelloWorld.o
        $(AR) r $(MYLIB) $?

clean:
        $(RM) $(MYLIB) 2>/dev/null
```

Listing A.15 contains familiar macro definitions, followed by the all target that depends on the lib target. As you can see, the lib target depends on three object files, and the command that is executed is the ar command that updates the library mylib.a with the three object files.

Now type the following command in a command shell:

```
make -f Makefile5 lib
```

The output is displayed here:

```
/usr/bin/ar r mylib.a FindChar2.o FindMain2.o HelloWorld.o
ar: creating archive mylib.a
```

Now type the following command:

```
make -f Makefile5 clean
```

The output is displayed here:

```
/bin/rm -f mylib.a 2>/dev/null
```

CREATING AN ARCHIVE LIBRARY IN A SHELL SCRIPT

You can also use a shell script createlib.sh to create a library that contains all the object files in the current directory, as shown here:

```
mylib2="mylib2.a"

for f in `ls *.o`
do
  echo "Adding object file $f"
  ar r $mylib2 $f
done
```

Open a command shell, navigate to the location of createlib.sh, and enter the following commands:

```
chmod +x createlib.sh
./createlib.sh
```

The output is shown here:

```
Adding object file FindChar2.o
ar: creating archive mylib2.a
Adding object file FindMain2.o
Adding object file HelloWorld.o
```

SUMMARY

This Appendix introduced you to the make utility and how to use this utility to automate compilation-related steps for your C programs. You saw how to use Unix commands for managing object files and libraries, such as the ar command and the ranlib commands. Then you learned about the nm command to examine the contents of object files and archive libraries.

Next, you saw how to create simple targets in a Makefile as well as how to use macros in a Makefile. In addition, you learned how to specify header files and library files in a Makefile, as well as how to invoke the make utility inside a Makefile. Finally, you learned how to create a shell script for creating an archive library.

INDEX